Photographing Tennis

I0493759

· **CHRIS NICHOLSON** ·

A Guide for Photographers, Parents, Coaches & Fans

Sidelight Books – Connecticut
2012

Cover design by Kirsten Navin, www.kirstennavin.com

All photographs and illustrations by Chris Nicholson

Editorial assistance: Jill Taussig, J. Broad and Catherine Johnson

Back-cover author portrait by Elizabeth Cecere

Printed in the United States of America

First Printing, 2012

ISBN 978-0-9835038-1-1

Sidelight Books
Connecticut, USA

www.PhotographingTennis.com

DEDICATION

To Mom and Dad, who on a warm evening in 1976, on a dead-end road on a Navy base in Charleston, South Carolina, taught me about tennis.

ACKNOWLEDGMENTS

Thank you to Ron Waite, who gave me the idea for this book.

Thank you to Lori, Lynne and Kirsten, the mid-1990s art and design staff of Tennis magazine. I mostly didn't know what I was doing. They encouraged me anyway.

Finally, thank you to my girlfriend Molly, who suggested that I thank her.

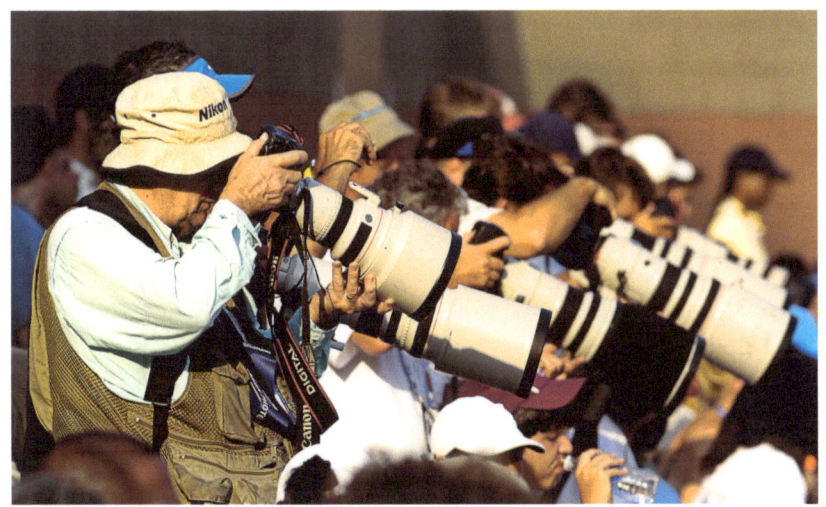

CONTENTS

Photographing
Tennis

Introduction

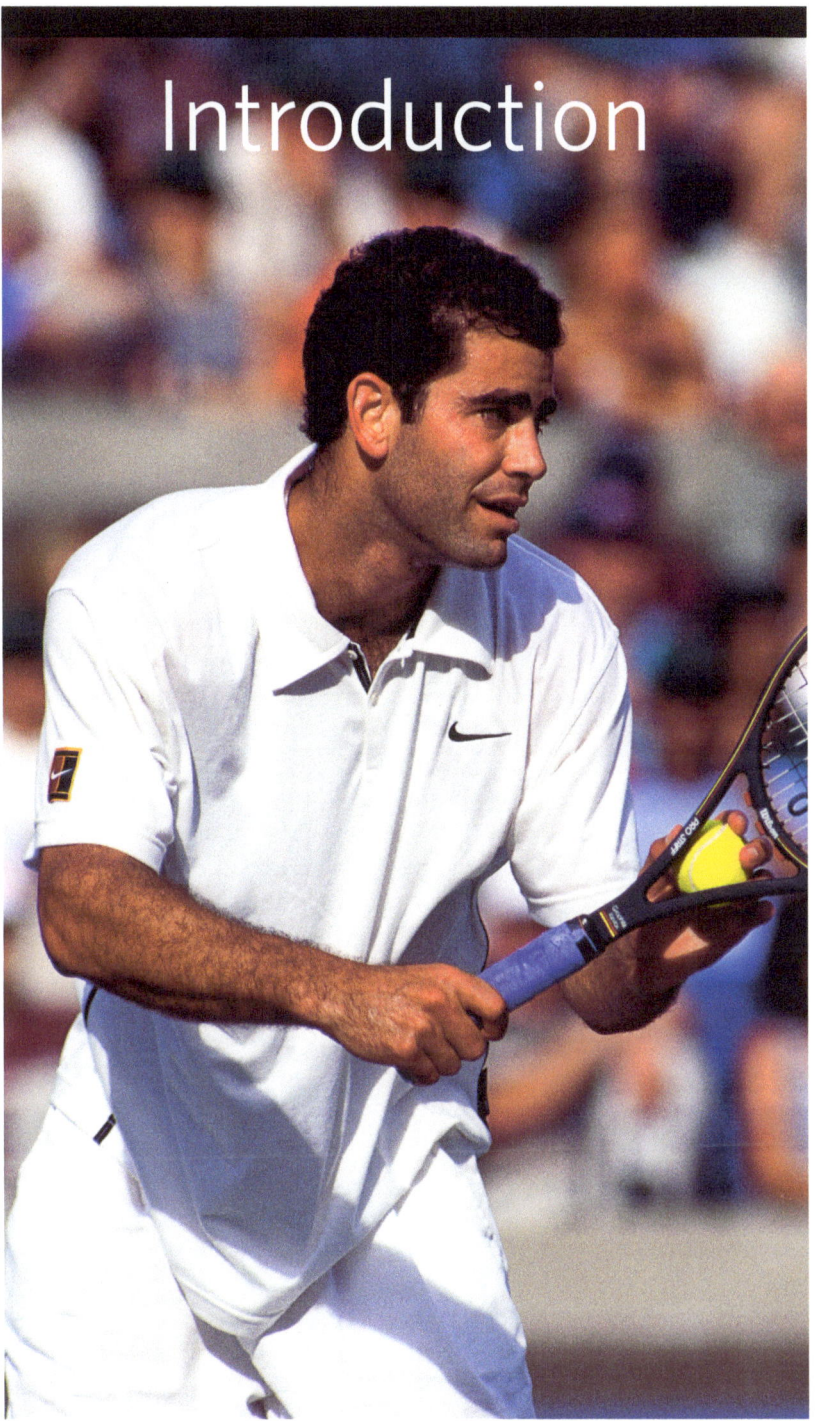

PHOTOGRAPHING TENNIS

I started photographing tennis in July 1995, while working as a researcher and writer at Tennis magazine. My first assignment was to cover Monica Seles at the Special Olympics in New Haven, Connecticut. She was there to guide the athletes through clinics, to award medals during official presentations, and to announce that she was returning to the pro tour two years after being stabbed by a spectator. I was thrilled to be covering such a big moment for the biggest tennis publication in the United States.

For my first photo of a professional tennis player, I sat in the stands (the wrong place). I shot with a short telephoto zoom (the wrong lens). The camera I used was too slow and too loud (other photographers kept looking around to see where the noise was coming from). Still, the photo appeared in the magazine, and I was paid.

Shortly thereafter I covered the tour events in New Haven; Pinehurst, North Carolina; Philadelphia; Newport; and then the US Open in New York City. For the first couple of years, I still didn't know much about what I was trying to do. I learned by making many mistakes, by studying my few successes, and by sitting next to pros whose work I respected while subtly trying to figure out what they were up to.

Sixteen years later I'm sitting in a café in Queens finishing a book about what I've learned. My hope is that I can help others enjoy photographing this great game, whether 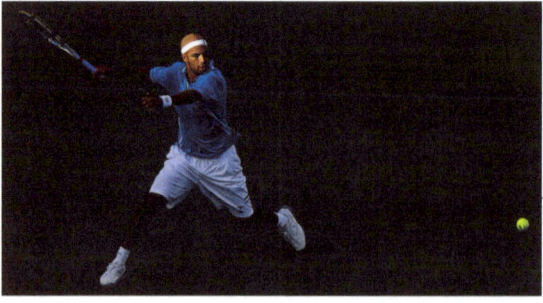 they're fellow professionals who want to learn a new niche, enthusiasts who love bringing a camera to a pro tournament, coaches who want to document the progress of their students, or parents who just want to make better pictures of their kids. Photography is another way to enjoy tennis, and I hope I can help you do it better.

Whichever category of photography you hail from, I can promise you this: Producing good tennis action photos involves a little luck. You use experience and knowledge to point the camera in the right direction and to open the shutter at the right time, and you hope what happens on court at that thousandth of a second works as a photograph. The luck is yours to find. The experience is yours to develop. The knowledge, I hope, you either get or enhance from this book.

Of course, other strategies exist for photographing tennis. I'm not saying this is the only way to shoot. It's just how I've been successful doing it. Some of what I lay forth in the following pages is a matter of judgment and opinion, but much could definitely be termed as "best practices." Either way, all my advice aims for perfection — not images that are just good enough, but ones that are the best you can do.

I'm also not saying this is easy. At the recreational, college and pro levels, I've also photographed basketball, football, golf, baseball, softball, wrestling, lacrosse, volleyball, track, soccer, surfing, hockey (ice and field), and rifling. But even after covering tennis for 16 years, I still find it the most difficult sport to shoot well. It's also, for me, the most rewarding.

CHAPTER ONE

Professionalism

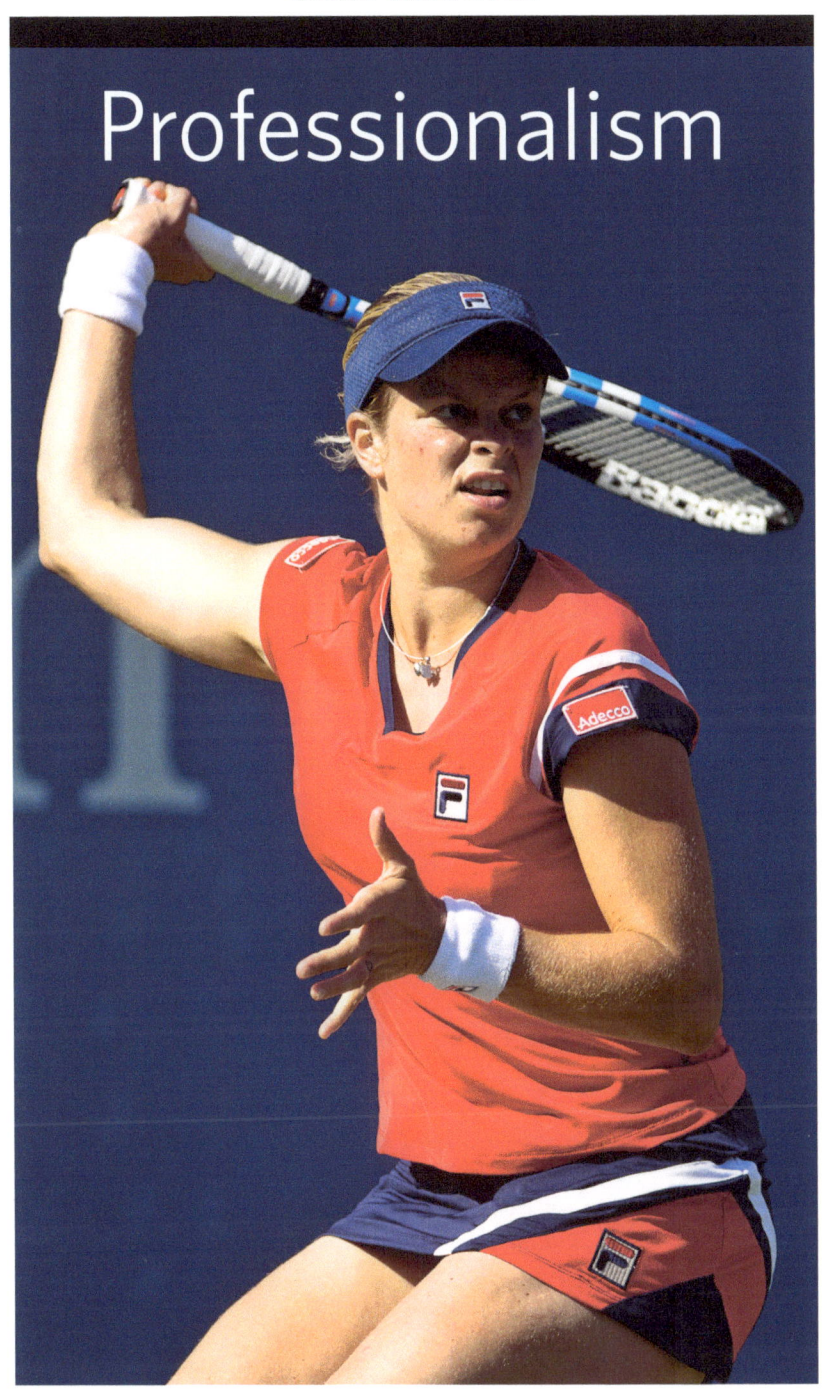

PROFESSIONALISM

Before learning techniques for photographing tennis, it's important to know how to *go about* photographing tennis. And then it's important to know how to go about circulating the images you make, if that's what you choose to do.

Here (and throughout this book), I use the word "professionalism" not in the sense of whether you make money with your images. In common usage this term has developed a connotation of expert-level skill, experience and judgement, along with a demeanor that encompasses those qualities. That connotation is what's important to this discussion. I'm not concerned about whether your images generate your income; that's not an adequate barometer for how good a photographer you are. Instead, this chapter is about appreciating and exhibiting a certain conduct for shooting tennis.

BEHAVIOR AND COURTESIES

Etiquette guides photographers when covering any sport, whether at the amateur or the professional level. Some sports (such as golf) have very restrictive guidelines. Other sports are a little looser in how they expect sideline-based photographers to go about their business. Tennis falls closer to the strict end of that spectrum.

The reason is one of focus (the players', not yours). Like golf, tennis is a game that requires a good amount of honed concentration and predictable lines of sight and sound. Players can be easily distracted by unexpected stimuli, especially when serving. I once accidentally tripped my shutter in the middle of Pete Sampras' service toss during an indoor match in Philadelphia. I was a good 30 feet away from him, yet he abandoned his motion, caught the ball, took a step off the baseline, put his chin down, scrunched his eyebrows and glared at me. I wanted to run out to him and explain that the noise was an accident, but that's also against the rules.

Fortunately, we don't have to guess how we're expected to act when shooting tennis. It's written down for us. How it got to be that way involves some relatively interesting bits of sports-photography history that starts before I was born.

Code of Conduct

In the late 1960s, tennis was entering its Open Era, and popularity of the game began to soar. Simultaneously, as you would expect, media interest in the sport began to grow. According to Russ Adams, one of the leading tennis photographers of that era (and a few eras thereafter—in fact, he was inducted into the International Tennis Hall of Fame in 2007), only 17 photographers requested a media credential for the 1968 US Open. The number grew to 56 in 1969, and then that number doubled in 1970. (Now about 350 photographers annually file applications.)

But photographers of the 60s faced a problem: Before tennis' popularity boomed, they were relegated to shooting from the top of the stands—*if* empty seats were available. The result was that most tennis photos looked the same: relatively static images made from a high aerial angle almost exclusively with telephoto lenses (which were somewhat inadequate for such work at the time, compared to the quality of glass that's available now). A fan with a good ticket could potentially make better photos than the pro photographers who were covering the event in an official capacity.

The photographers solved this problem by banding together and collectively requesting that tournaments place

One of the most important times in tennis for the photographer to be silent and "invisible" is when a player is preparing to serve.

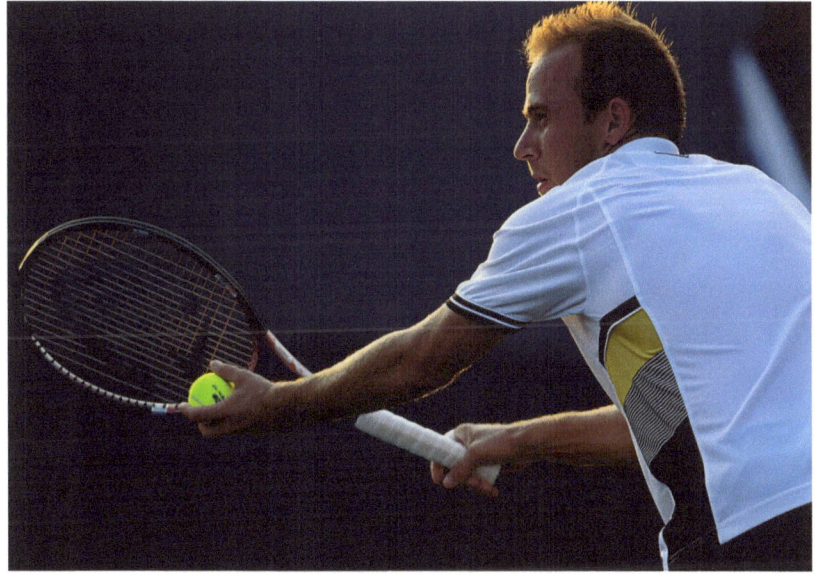

them courtside. In exchange, the photographers drafted, negotiated and agreed to a set of rules they would follow. These rules, published in book form, were known as the "Code of Conduct."

The code has changed little since. It doesn't exist in such a highly official form nowadays, but the guidelines governing photographers' behavior are relatively consistent for each tournament. (See the Appendix for more information.)

When it comes to acting professionally, you may ask: Do I need to know this if I'm not a professional photographer? Do I need to know this code if I'm not shooting pro players? The answer is yes. If you act professionally, you're more likely to be treated with respect, and you're less likely to draw negative attention from players, officials or security. Even if you're shooting only amateur players, you will be almost invisible on court—and this is the most important reason for the entire code of conduct.

The breakdown of behavior expected from tennis photographers is as follows:

The very best tournaments have courtside seating reserved for credentialed photographers.

STAY QUIET

Keep silent in every way you can imagine. Don't talk, don't rattle equipment around, don't needlessly rapid-fire loud shutters, and keep your cell phone off. Do not talk to

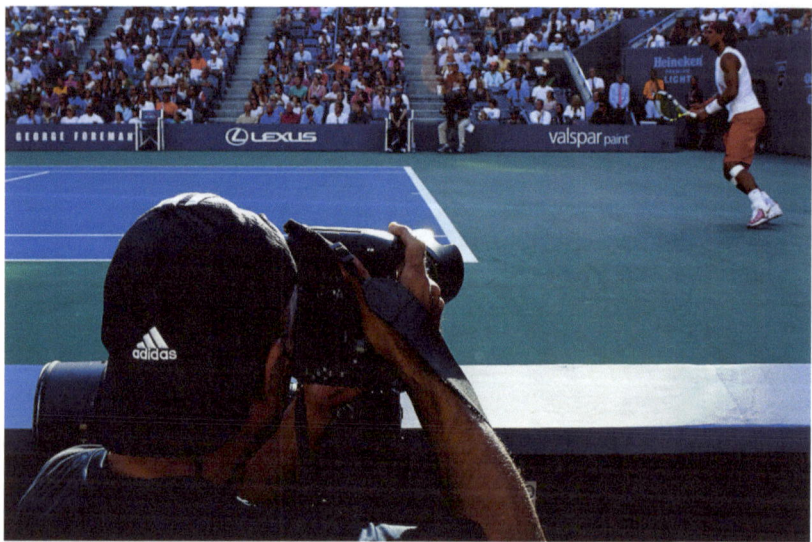

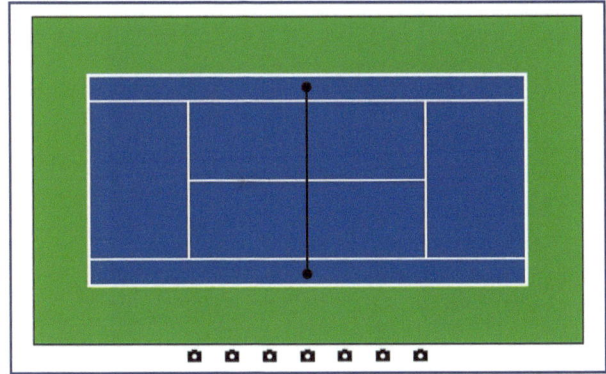

Figure 1
Most organized
tournaments will
allow photogra-
phers to position
themselves, at a
minimum, to the
side of the court
between the two
baselines.

players, do not talk to officials, do not talk to chair umpires and lines judges, and do not talk to court attendants.

STAY PUT

Do not move during games, and definitely do not move during points. If your angle is bad, if a ballkid stands in front of you, if you need to use the restroom, if you need to leave and call someone to see if you should buy milk on the way home — *wait for the changeover.*

STAY IN YOUR PLACE

Organized tournaments will likely have specific spots where photographers are allowed to shoot. In stringent circumstances, this will be along the side of the court and between the service lines (see Figure 1). Larger pro tournaments will usually have a designated "photo pit" for credentialed photographers (i.e., those with a press pass) that stretches from baseline to baseline on one or both sides of the court. Very large pro tournaments may also grant photographers access to other areas, such as windowed dugouts behind the backscreen (such as at the US Open), or catwalks above covered or partially-covered courts (Australian Open).

Staying in these approved positions is important for several reasons, the most important of which is psychological conditioning. Tennis players (especially pros) learn, if even subconsciously, where the photographers will be stationed. Therefore, players learn to mentally block out the cameras' presence, and even the cameras' noise. If they see or hear a photographer (or an official, or a spectator, or security)

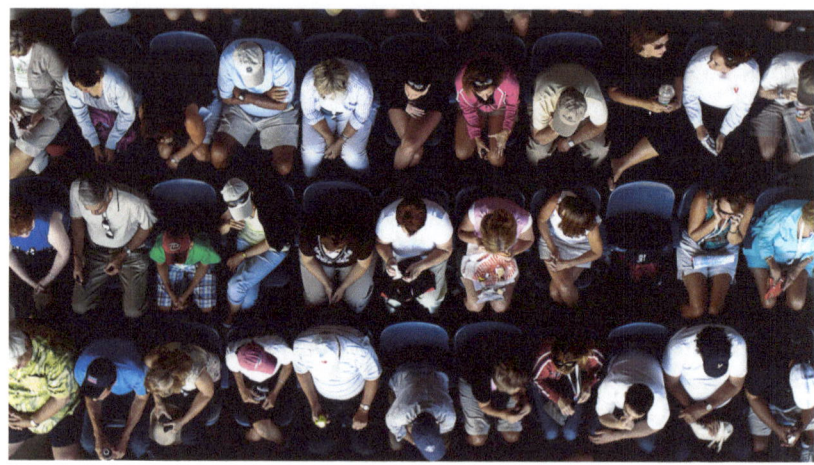

Spectators (whether on site or watching on TV) are how professional events make money. To stay in good graces with the tournament, never obstruct fans or a television camera.

in an unexpected place, the players can become distracted mid-point. That's never fun for anyone involved.

If you are granted court access at an event, pro or amateur, and you don't know for sure where you're permitted to shoot in that venue, then ask. Start with the event's media contact; if you can't find him or her, ask a tournament referee or director, or ask security, or ask a court official. If you don't know for sure that you are allowed on court (and you won't be allowed on court at a pro event, unless you have a credential), then you should stay off.

And never, ever, ever block a television camera.

STAY OBJECTIVE

Do not applaud. Do not cheer. Even if you are producing a Pulitzer-winning image that you know will make you hundreds of thousands of dollars, even if you are photographing your only child winning a junior Grand Slam final—if you have been allowed to photograph from an official position, then be professionally objective throughout the match.

STAY RESPECTFUL

When you're working next to other photographers, be mindful that they also have work to do. This is especially important if you're shooting for fun or portfolio and the photographers around you are shooting for a salary. Allow adequate space for others to work; if you're shooting shoulder-to-shoulder in different directions, this sometimes means one of you will have to "shoot low" and the other "shoot high"—in other words, one of you shoots over the other's lens, and vice versa. If you're positioned so close to another photographer that your shoulders are touching, be careful not to bump or jostle his or her camera.

Also important is to remember to be respectful of spectators. At a pro event (and perhaps even at an amateur one) they have paid to watch. As long as they're occupying a legitimate viewpoint, let them do so unimpeded.

STAY STROBELESS

Never use a flash when photographing a tennis match. A flash can very easily distract tennis players and officials, and it can also interfere with a spectator's vision. A flash going off during a point is grounds for the chair umpire calling a let; if you're responsible for stoppage of play and the cancellation of a point, you may be asked to leave the court. You can get away with flash photography after the final point of the match, but even then it can be frowned upon.

VALUE YOUR WORK

A mark of professionalism, even if you're not a full-time photographer, is internalizing the idea that your photos have value.

Don't Give Away Photos

If you ask any independent sports photographer how the market has changed in the first decade of the 21st century, he or she will fill the next few hours of your life with stories of price plummets caused by the Internet, worldwide accessibility, web theft, low-balling global agencies, aggressive contract lawyers, dishonest clients and so on. Technology has changed almost the entire photography market (especially the sports niche) in ways that are almost certainly irreversible. Camera gear is more expensive and depreciates drastically and quickly, while clients value the product less under the illusion that digital photos are easy and cheap to produce. Additionally, cameras are far superior to what was available even a few years ago, making the production of average images an accessible skill to people with a wider range of talent. High-quality photos are still difficult to produce, which is good news for the best photographers. But increasingly smaller creative budgets means that a majority of buyers are choosing from an over-saturated market of mediocre images, and paying cheaply for them.

However, that doesn't mean that photos have no value. One of the causes of the downward trend in the market has been photographers allowing use of their images for little or no compensation. Don't get caught in this trap. Even if you're not calling photography your profession, just the fact that you're reading this book means that you are willing to put some work into taking better tennis photos. That work is worth something, especially if a third party wants to use your images to promote themselves or their business.

If newspapers, magazines, websites, agents, manufacturers, associations and so on discover that you produce decent tennis photography, they may want to use it. Many may offer you no money, and will perhaps even try to woo you by promising to print your name alongside your work. Bylines are fun and have value, but they don't buy new lenses, they don't buy extra hard drive space, they don't pay travel expenses, and banks don't accept them as deposits. Besides, a publication should run your name with your photo anyway, in addition to paying you. Don't let yourself be fooled — photography is valued by publications and other businesses, and they will pay you for it if they know you expect to be paid.

If you have any thought of ever making money with your photographs, see the Appendix of this book for links to information on good business practices.

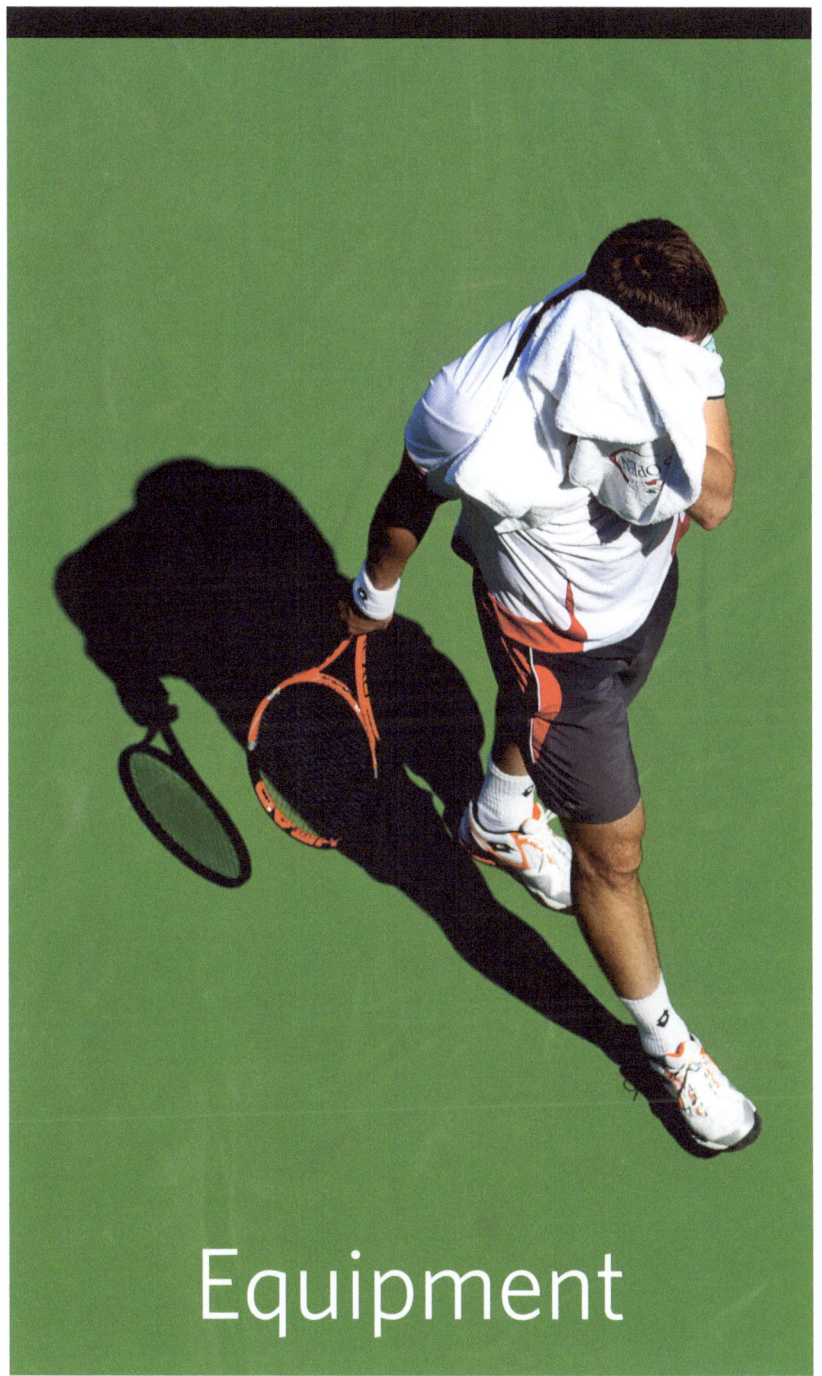

Equipment

EQUIPMENT

I once sat at a father-of-friend's house and listened to my host pontificate about the pro-photography "scam." He didn't know my occupation, but I'm not sure that knowledge would have curbed his comments. He lectured about how the only difference between professional photographers and dabblers was the quality of their gear. "The fancy camera does all the work," he said, "and then these frauds charge thousands of dollars just to hold it in front of you."

He was wrong, but did speak one grain of truth: Gear makes a difference. A $5,000 camera with an $8,000 lens won't make you Ansel Adams, but it will allow you to work better if you know how to wield its advantages.

The relevant application of that anecdote is this: You don't need to use the most expensive and the best camera available. However, if you buy the best gear you can afford, you'll be thankful once you're on court.

What makes a better camera "better"? A few qualities:

- It's built better — it's more durable. It's not made with cheap plastic parts that break when put through frequent or tough use.

- The autofocus is faster and more accurate. This means that at the end of a shoot, more photos will be in focus and less will be in the trash.

- Accessing the functions is easier. Important settings are quicker to activate and alter — they're not hidden within layers of menu options, nor activated with a complicated series of button pushes and wheel turns. Never underestimate the importance of a simple workflow.

- It reacts better. When you trip the shutter, it takes a picture nearly instantaneously.

- The image files are better. (Not bigger, necessarily. Just better quality.)

One final note before we move on to specifics: As you're already seeing, I'm assuming you're shooting with a digital camera, and will therefore limit this discussion appropriately. If you'd like to shoot film, I applaud you. Use Fuji Velvia 50 in bright sunlight, expose it at 80, push-process it one stop, and skip all my advice specific to digital gear.

CAMERAS

The first piece of equipment you need is, of course, a camera. Which model you use is more important in the digital world than it was with film. It used to be that a camera was just the conduit between light and emulsion. But now the camera contains the actual medium, i.e., the sensor. That piece is the foundation for all the other photographic tools that follow.

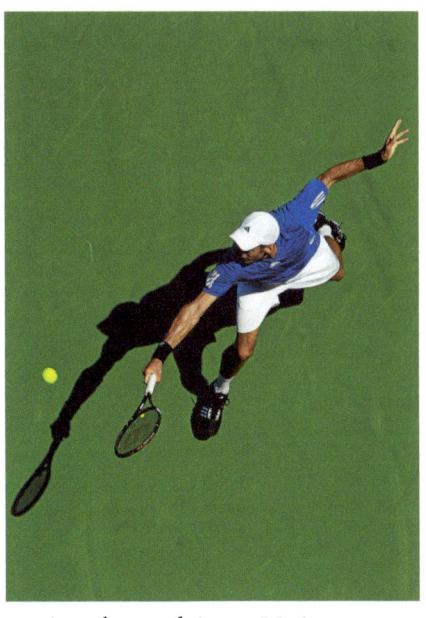

Modern cameras can produce an amazing number of pixels, but that may not be worth a high price if you don't need them all. The cover photo for this book was made with a 12MP camera; 24MP would have been overkill.

Resolution

Just about any real camera (by "real," I mean one that's not part of a phone) you can buy today has more than enough resolution to make good photos. I shoot with a 12-megapixel (MP) camera, which, in a practical analysis, serves me no better or worse than a 10MP or 24MP camera would. Megapixels are mainly a marketing tool that manufacturers use to make new cameras sound better than old ones. Why do extra megapixels not always make a difference? For two main reasons:

1. All pixels are not created equal. When it comes to sensor chips, more important than resolution are color accuracy, contrast, sharpness (as introduced by the camera, not the lens), and highlight and shadow detail. Also, a difference exists between CCD and CMOS sensors. And large sensors (in

terms of physical size, not pixel density) are almost always better than small. (The reason for all this is beyond the scope of this book. If you're interested in why one is different and/or better than the other, I encourage you to research the topic online. The answer can be found, among other places, in the resources listed in the Appendix.)

2. You don't need many pixels to create a quality photograph. Besides, despite common assumptions, a 12MP photo is not twice the physical size of a 6MP photo. It's only 40 percent larger.

I'm not saying that resolution doesn't matter. It does. It just stops mattering much after a certain point, depending on how you want to use your photos. Disposing of theory and moving to specifics, the minimum target resolutions I recommend for some different uses are:

Prints up to 6x9", web, book and newspaper	5MP
Prints up to 8x12", magazine	9MP
Small poster prints	12MP
Large poster prints	20MP

(Resolutions higher than 20MP do offer advantages in some photo niches, just not ones that most photographers work

Diffraction Limits

A rather advanced (and obscure) topic in photography these days revolves around the fact that the cells in digital sensors have become so tiny that lenses set to small apertures cannot accurately focus light into them. The result is that when shooting with a closed-down lens, you actually lose resolution in your images. Your 12MP camera would effectively become 6MP just because you shoot at f/11.

However, this issue hardly ever affects the tennis photographer. For most cameras, the effect isn't seen until the aperture gets smaller than f/8 — which you'll almost never use for shooting high-speed action.

in.) This is not a comprehensive guide to ideal resolutions, but rather just enough info to cover the most common uses of photos. (For information on other needs, the web contains almost limitless assistance.) So what does matter more than resolution? Technique. Technique is far more important to image quality than resolution is. Much of the information in the rest of this book can help the former compensate for a lack in the latter.

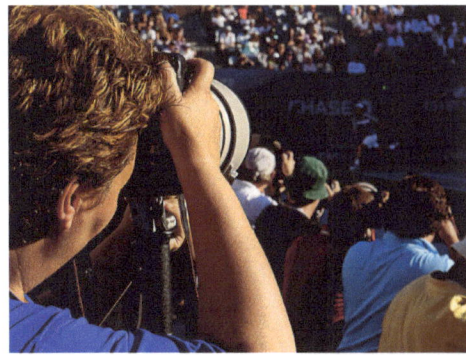

Quality cameras are worth the price for several reasons, among them the miniscule shutter lag that is required for accurately timing action photos.

Format

Discussing resolution begs the question of sensor format. Which is best for tennis: full-frame (35mm), APS-C, Micro Four Thirds, or something else?

This I leave to personal preference. Each format has so many pros and cons that your choice will ultimately relate more to your style or comfort than to any dictum about what's "right." Full-frame sensors have more dynamic range, APS-C sensors allow for greater depth of field, Micro Four Thirds sensors come packaged in lighter cameras.

The camera I use has an APS-C sensor, which is 16x24mm. The result most important for me is that its image magnification is 1.5 times greater than a full-frame camera. I like this for tennis because it means I don't have to carry the biggest, heaviest lenses anymore. It also means I don't have to worry much about filters and lens hoods vignetting my images.

Shutter Lag

These days you can find professional features in many middle-range camera bodies, and even in some lower-range bodies. Just not all the features. The difference with a pro camera is that it contains everything a professional image-maker would probably want or need in one package.

While middle-range and even some lower-range camera bodies may be able to compete with pro bodies in some aspects, they can't compete in all.

One area where you'll find a notable difference, one that's important when it comes to photographing tennis, is shutter lag—the amount of time between when your finger presses the shutter release and when the camera actually records an image. (This assumes the frame is in focus when you press the button. Some manufacturers and testers include auto-focusing time in their shutter-lag measurements, which is unreasonable; they're two different mechanical specifications and should therefore be measured separately.)

Shutter lag is generally measured in milliseconds. Some cameras have shutter lags over 1,000 milliseconds (ms), or one second. These are essentially useless for good action photography in any sport. On the other hand, pro cameras usually feature shutter lag so short that it's imperceptible. That's one of the features that justifies their high price tags. Mid-range, or "prosumer," cameras (even very good ones) tend to have longer lags. Just for the sake of illustrating this point, here's a comparison of shutter lags in cameras of varying types:

Model	Type	Sh. Lag
Canon EOS-1D Mark IV	Pro	80ms
Canon EOS-1Ds Mark III	Pro	40ms
Leica M9	Pro	80ms
Nikon D2x	Pro	37ms
Nikon D3s	Pro	10ms
Olympus E5	Pro	10ms
Canon 400D Rebel XTi	Prosumer	100ms
Canon PowerShot SD95	Prosumer	64ms
Nikon D70	Prosumer	124ms
Olympus D540	Prosumer	190ms
Canon G12	Pocket	380ms
Nikon Coolpix L3	Pocket	180ms

As you can see, better cameras generally record an image more quickly. But not always. So if you're not planning to

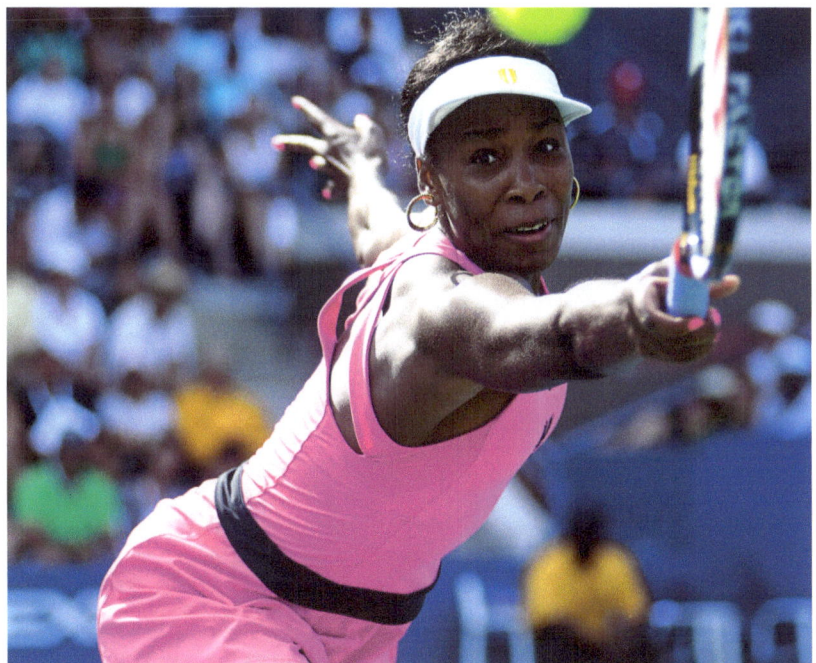

use a top-of-the-line model, then do some research to find a camera that's better than others in this area.

Why? As you may have already concluded, shutter lag affects timing, and timing is a critical element in shooting tennis. (Critical enough that a whole chapter of this book is devoted to the topic.) When you decide that what you see in your viewfinder would make a good photograph and you push the shutter release, you want to know that your camera can capture that moment before it's over. In tennis, that time window is in milliseconds. Therefore, the shorter the shutter lag, the better.

How fast is best? That probably varies from person to person, but I can tell you this: In the film days, I shot tennis with a Nikon F5, which boasted a shutter lag of 40ms. To my perception, this felt instantaneous. Then when Nikon released the D1x with its 72ms shutter lag, my timing was dramatically affected—I was missing so many shots that within two days I reverted back to shooting film. I just couldn't use the D1x to reliably photograph tennis. When Nikon released the D2x with its 37ms shutter lag, the timing felt right again. Part of this is conditioning; I was accustomed

Capturing fast bursts of action requires not only good reflexes, but a camera that responds even faster than you do.

Figure 2
In the example of an autofocus system with only one sensor (left), you cannot aim at the player's eyes while keeping them along a rule-of-thirds line. However, with multiple sensors (right) you can select a higher focus point that allows you to keep good composition and ideal focus simultaneously.

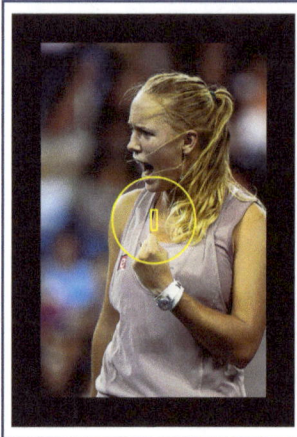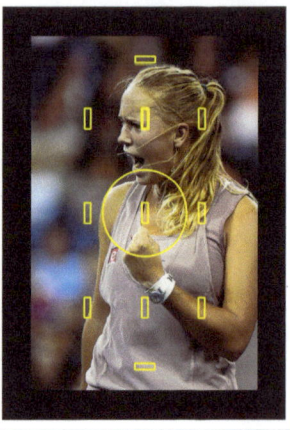

to a certain reflex in my camera and had a hard time adjusting to double the delay. But part was simply mechanics: The shorter shutter lag your camera has, the better your tennis action photos will be.

If you find that your camera's shutter lag is long enough to negatively affect your timing, what can you do? You have two options: Buy a faster camera, or improve your anticipation.

Autofocus

Is autofocus critical to photographing tennis? The answer is no. As proof, I offer the fact that photographers were successfully shooting tennis long before any camera could focus well on its own. Photographers learned and perfected the art of continually focusing their lenses by hand as a second sense — they didn't have to think about focusing, they just focused.

That's how I started, too, in the early 1990s. And it's how I kept shooting until about three months into my professional career, when I bought cameras that focused better and faster than my hand could. Though I could manually focus well, when I started using a good autofocus, my rate of successful frames improved immediately.

So let me adjust my answer to the question: No, you don't need autofocus, but it sure helps. When choosing a camera, definitely test its autofocus capability. It should:

- **Focus quickly.** The quicker, the better. If the camera takes too long to lock onto the subject, you will miss action photos.

- **Focus definitively.** The autofocus should adjust and lock in what feels like one step. If you can see and/or hear the elements waffling between focus points, then you're not using an autofocus system that's adequate for sports photography.

- **Track well.** "Focus tracking" is when the camera has locked onto a moving target and stays in focus while that subject moves closer or further away. This is important in tennis, a sport in which players hardly ever stay still. You want your camera to be able to keep its focus while a player moves around court; that way, when you're ready to shoot, the frame is already sharp. (Some cameras can identify what you want to keep in focus, and continue tracking even when the subject moves from the active focus sensor.)

While the camera's autofocus system is an important consideration, your lens choice can be just as important. Some lenses focus faster and better than others. Usually newer lenses are better, but some brands actually have different focusing technology built into lenses of varying values. For instance, Nikon's S-series lenses (the S signifies "Silent Wave") have built-in motors that assist the camera's focusing system, thereby accelerating the process.

Autofocus not only needs to be quick to lock onto its subject, but also needs to be good at tracking a moving target.

Another consideration with autofocus is the number of focus sensors. Some cameras use just one spot in the center of the frame to determine focus; some use a few sensors spread out around the frame (usually along the "Rule of Thirds"

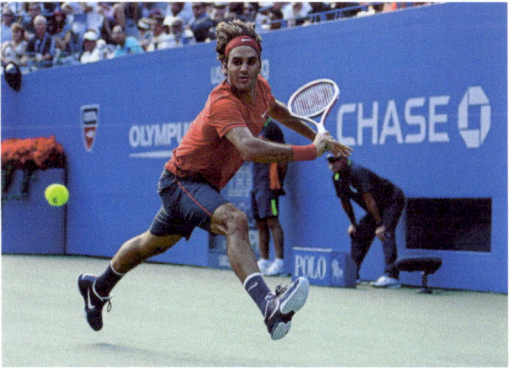

lines); and some have an inordinate number of sensors that provide incredibly (and perhaps unnecessarily) precise autofocus placement.

Which is best for tennis? The number of sensors doesn't matter, as long as it's more than one. The visual nature of tennis dictates that the point of required focus (usually the player's eyes) will almost never be in the center of a well-composed frame. Therefore, you want a camera that will allow you to focus at an off-center point, ideally along a line of thirds (see Figure 2). You also want a camera that will allow you to move your focus point easily and quickly. Most cameras put this control in a button on the back of the body, which is perfect.

One last point about autofocus regards how to activate it. Most (if not all) cameras will focus when you depress the shutter release halfway. However, a growing trend is to deactivate that feature and instead use a dedicated AF button (usually on the back of the body) to activate the autofocus. This allows you to compose a frame, focus and then move on to other concerns—when you eventually press the shutter release, the camera will not change the focus.

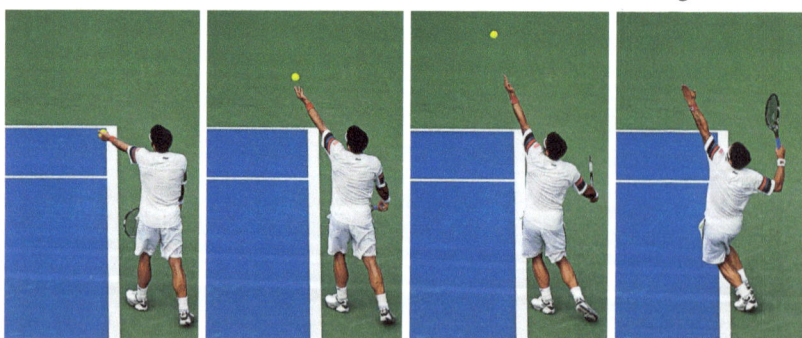

Which technique is better for shooting tennis? The former is. People are different, so you may find that the dedicated button works better for you; when I'm shooting anything other than sports, I use the dedicated button. But when I'm photographing tennis or any other action sport, I find that continually holding my thumb to the back of the camera induces cramps after about 15 minutes. I can only imagine how it would feel after 10 hours of matches.

Also, as mentioned previously, you want to constantly stay in focus when shooting action. So if you're thumbing down a button on the back of the camera, you need to simultaneously use your finger to push the shutter release; you're asking your mind to independently control two actions at once, which invariably changes your grip (which could change your framing). Therefore, it's best to use the half-depressed shutter to focus—then you're primed to fully depress when you want to capture a photograph. One finger, one button, two purposes; one stone, two birds. It will make your actions quicker and more fluid.

Frame Rate

When you push the shutter release of a digital camera, the processor gathers all the pertinent information it needs to make a photograph, opens the shutter, reads an exposure from the sensor, sends the exposure data to the processor which in turn writes the image file to the memory card, and closes the shutter. The number of times a camera can do that in one second is its "frame rate." In other words, how many times in one second can the camera take a picture?

If you want to shoot sequences, your camera needs to be able to record a high number of frames per second (in this case, eight).

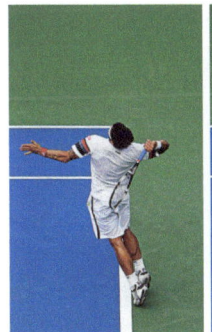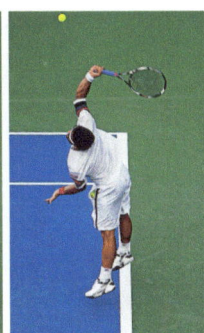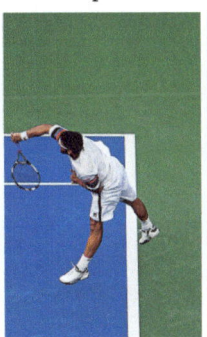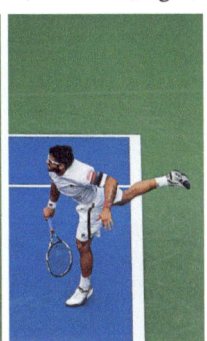

To Burst or Not

Sports photographers generally employ one of two strategies: 1) During play, hold down the shutter release to record a rapid-fire burst of frames, or 2) wait for a specific moment, then shoot one or two targeted slices of the action. The first method generates a lot of files, and because of the random nature of the timing, many will be throwaways. However, you're sure to get some usable frames. The second method produces fewer photos, but the few you do make will have a higher chance of being good.

Which is better? It's your choice. At the end of a day I tend to produce just as many quality photos using either strategy. But I prefer the selective approach. Why? Because by choosing my moments, I have less junk to sift through, and I feel like I'm *creating* my images rather than lucking into them.

In tennis photography, this specification is important to varying degrees. The variable, of course, is your style of shooting. If you tend to strategize when you're going to open the shutter, planning each photo and waiting to expose frames one at a time, then you probably don't care much what your frame rate is. (That's what I usually do.) But if you like to shoot bursts of frames, or if you like to shoot high-speed sequences of action, then frame rate will be among your concerns when choosing a camera.

Tennis strokes happen fast — about a second from preparing a stroke to following through after impact. So to get a good sequence, you'll need a minimum of six frames per second. If you want to shoot a full, detailed sequence, you'll want at least ten frames per second. (The shutter noise generated by bodies with even higher frame rates can be a nuisance, necessitating the use of what's known as a sound blimp — a sound-damping enclosure for the camera.)

Unlike other camera specs, frame rate is hard to claim an ideal for. Much will depend on your style and your wants and expectations. If in doubt, over-compensate; cameras with high frame rates often grant the option for slower shooting, so you can customize the effect.

A final point to consider is that your frame rate will be affected by your camera's autofocus capability. If your camera can't predict, find and lock focus quickly, then either your frame rate will decelerate or your focus will be less accurate. Therefore, if the ability to shoot rapid bursts is important to you, then topnotch autofocus should be, too.

Point & Shoots

You want to use a single-lens reflex (SLR) camera when shooting tennis. Can you use a point-and-shoot camera? Can you use a pocket camera? Yes. But you want to use an SLR when shooting tennis.

Point-and-shoot cameras have gotten much better in just the past couple of years. Some (such as the Canon G1x and the Olympus E-P3) produce professional-quality files. But they're not meant for photographing sports on a serious level. (That doesn't mean you can't use them. Modern professional tennis players shouldn't use wood racquets, but I once saw Pete Sampras hit a 125-m.p.h. serve with one. Again: Technique is more important than gear.)

If you want or need to use a pocket camera, just be sure:

• It has an optical zoom (not digital zoom) with good reach (ideally you want the lens to zoom to at least a 200mm equivalent).

• It allows you to manually set your exposure, or to at least set exposure compensation (more on this in Chapter 4).

• It allows you to turn off the flash (see "Code of Conduct" in Chapter 1).

• It meets the technical specifications discussed earlier in this chapter (resolution, shutter lag and autofocus).

Know Your Camera

No matter what camera you use—whether a $7,500 professional DSLR or a $250 point-and-shoot—be sure to understand its features and limitations. Read the manual.

Play with the settings. Practice until operating the camera is second nature. You want to know it so well that you can adjust settings without having to think about which button to push or which wheel to turn. You should be able to just do it.

LENSES

A camera is like a brain; a lens is like an eye. You want the best eyes possible. In fact, I would argue that a beginning photographer buy top-of-the-line lenses before buying a top-of-the-line camera. The priority in acquiring lenses for photographing tennis is as follows:

TELEPHOTO

In particular, you want, at minimum, the equivalent of a 200mm lens. 300mm is better, and perhaps as close to perfect as you can get. 400mm is also excellent, but terrifically more expensive. If you can afford them, 500mm and 600mm lenses also have courtside value.

But if you're going to splurge on one telephoto lens, or if you're looking for a place to start a telephoto collection, then get a 300mm. That length is ideal for most of the tennis-photography scenarios you'll come across, even more so with a sub-35mm sensor. With this lens you can get close enough to the action to fill the frame, but not so close that you crop off needed body parts.

At the 2011 US Open, I shot 74 percent of my photos with a 300mm f/2.8. However, note that I shoot with a Nikon D2x camera, which has a magnification factor of 1.5 (see "35mm Equivalents" on page 24). Therefore, when I shoot with a 300mm, I'm shooting with a 450mm equivalent. I do this deliberately (rather than using Nikon's current flagship, the D4) because, for almost the same net effect, I reduce my tennis-photography lens overhead by over $3,000 and my

A telephoto lens (here, a 600mm) allows you to magnify the scene and get close to the action.

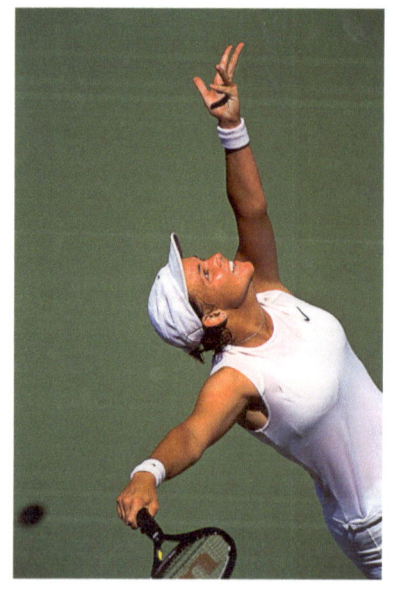

payload by nearly four pounds. (Though the former reason may seem more important, I actually care more about the latter. Big glass becomes quite unwieldy in a tournament environment.)

Even better than a fixed-length telephoto is a quality telephoto zoom lens. Perhaps the best tennis lens ever made is the 200-400mm f/4 (made by both Canon and Nikon). It allows just about a full range of the coverage needed to shoot full-frame compositions regardless of your position and the player's location on court.

A short-telephoto zoom is ideal if you want to fill the frame with a full-body photo.

SHORT-TELEPHOTO ZOOM

Telephoto lenses are expensive, but don't fret—a next-best option is available. A zoom lens that covers the range of normal to short-telephoto (such as a 70-200mm) will prove a versatile option when photographing tennis. Depending on where you're positioned, having such a lens along with a 300mm will allow you to create just about every type of tennis photo you can think of. (Or, look into the Sigma 120-300mm f/2.8.)

However, be aware that zooms tend to produce more flare than fixed-length

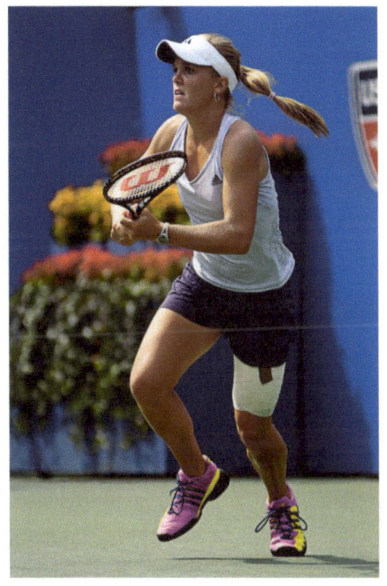

35mm Equivalents

In the digital age, photography has been presented with an issue similar to that of light bulbs in the 1990s. Previously, as a society, we had grown accustomed to relating an incandescent light bulb's wattage with its brightness, even though the relationship between the two was circumstantial. In other words, we knew approximately how bright any 75-watt bulb would be. Then those spiral-shaped fluorescent bulbs came to market. The latter use less energy to create equivalent brightness — a 20-watt fluorescent produces about the same amount of light as a 75-watt incandescent. This created a problem for consumers accustomed to 20-watt bulbs being dim. To combat this predisposition, manufacturers printed an "equivalent" wattage on the fluorescent bulb's package so that people would understand how bright the bulb would be.

How does this relate to camera lenses? A 200mm lens is a 200mm lens. The number — the "focal length" — indicates the distance between the front element and the camera's sensor. The higher the number, the higher the magnification of the lens. In the film era, when most people were using 35mm format, a 200mm lens resulted in the same magnification on just about everyone's camera. However, the digital age has brought us a variety of commonly used formats, all of which alter a lens' magnification effect (or the "effective angle of view").

For example, the Canon EOS 5D's full-frame sensor is 36mm wide and the Canon EOS 20D camera's sensor is 22mm wide. The difference has an effect on the image produced by the same lens mounted on each camera; the 20D's sensor magnifies the effective angle of view to 1.6 times more than the 5D's sensor (a magnification factor indicated as "1.6x"). Therefore, a 200mm on the 5D produces the same effect as it did on any 35mm film camera that came before. However, the same lens on the 20D, because the image is being focused on a smaller sensor, has the effect that we would normally expect from a 320mm lens (200mm x 1.6 = 320mm). Therefore, a 200mm lens used on the 20D would be a "320mm equivalent."

Why the quirky terminology? Because it reduces focal lengths to a common denominator — it allows us to describe a lens not by its size, but by its behavior. If I suggest using a 200mm lens, that may not be a specific enough suggestion, because that could create different results for different cameras. But if I suggested using 200mm-equivalent, that would relay a precise intended result. However, that gets a little wordy. So in this book I'll generally just refer to a focal length. If I write "200mm," I mean the 35mm equivalent of a 200mm.

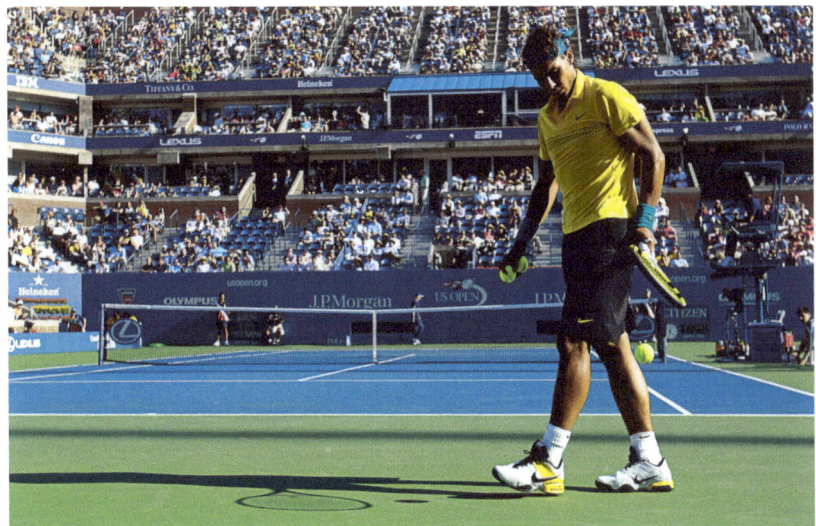

lenses. This can be a problem when shooting back-lit, when the sun might be pointing right into your front element. But that occasional annoyance is far outweighed by the ability to change your framing while tracking a player around the court. Moreover, flare can usually be prevented by employing a lens hood (see page 30), or even by using your hand or a hat to block the sun.

A wide-angle lens can help you illustrate tennis in a way not usually seen.

WIDE-ANGLE

Once while shooting a big tournament, a veteran tennis photographer told me, "Most of these photographers wouldn't know what the [bad word] to do with a wide-angle lens." His point was a tad overstated but contained some truth: Shooting wide in tennis is not easy. Some tennis photographers don't ever put a wide-angle lens on the camera, and they therefore miss some tremendous creative opportunities. So you might consider carrying a zoom lens that covers a range of wide to normal, such as a 17-55mm.

Though using a wide-angle lens might seem intuitive, it can take time to master. The common issue is that controlling the background becomes even harder, simply because there's more background to control.

Another trouble area is that the idea behind using a wide-angle lens is not necessarily to include more of the scene, but to get closer to your subject. As we already know, getting

A Teleconverter Pro

Though I hardly ever use my 1.4x teleconverter, it does provide an additional improvement to shooting with a D2x. This camera, as previously mentioned, has a 1.5x magnification factor, which makes my 300mm f/2.8 the equivalent of a 450mm f/2.8. When I add the converter, I'm carrying what is essentially a 630mm f/4 that weighs only 6.8 pounds.

A 600mm f/4 weighs over 11 pounds. So the 600mm is almost twice as much in weight and over twice as expensive. If used with good technique, my TC-14E allows me to get nearly the same quality shooting experience while saving my bank account and my back some grief.

close to tennis action is not easy. I've had most of my success using wide-angle lenses when positioned courtside near the baseline, or when photographing from behind the court.

TELECONVERTERS

A teleconverter (or "extender") increases a lens' magnification by a fixed percentage, and can be a useful tool in tennis photography. One of its downfalls, however, is that it absorbs at least one stop of light. For example, a 1.4x teleconverter makes a 200mm f/2.8 lens act like a 280mm f/4; a 2.0x converter makes the same lens a 400mm f/5.6. The smaller aperture will force you toward slower shutter speeds, which is often counter to the needs of a sports photographer.

Therefore, loss of light is an important consideration when choosing an accompanying lens. Stated simply, you want to use a teleconverter only with fast lenses. A combination used by some photographers is a 200mm f/2 with a 1.4x converter, making a 280mm f/2.8 — a combination lighter and more portable than the nearly equivelent 300mm f/2.8. On the other hand, if you use a 2.0x with an f/4 lens, you have a minimum aperture of f/8. That's nice for landscapes, but in sports it means your shutter speed is slow and your autofocus is weak. (Many cameras' autofocus systems don't work well if they're receiving less light than allowed at f/5.6.)

You can, of course, compensate for the light loss by increasing your ISO. In the last example, you could get the shutter speed back by increasing your ISO two stops. However, that will reduce image quality (if even a little), compounding the teleconverter's other downfall: image degradation. The mere act of adding the converter's extra elements to your lens "roughs up" your image. Increasing your ISO is then like taking two sledgehammers to your photo quality rather than just the one. (In fact, I advise against using a 2.0x converter anyway; the best ever made still degrades image quality more than I like. I recall selling only one image ever that I made with a 2.0x converter.)

As you may have already surmised, this loss of light also makes it impractical to use a teleconverter with a variable-aperture lens. Many of these lenses open up to only f/5.6 on the far end. Thus, your maximum aperture with the converter becomes f/8 or f/11. What little light you had is therefore rendered nearly useless, plus you've hampered your autofocus.

Additionally, variable-aperture lenses are, by nature, zoom lenses. And teleconverters sometimes don't work with zooms. Either the optics don't match up properly, or the mechanics are dangerous to the glass (the converter could actually come in contact with the lens' rear element).

Another issue is motion blur. At high magnifications, even with fast shutter speeds, slightly moving the lens can blur the entire image. (You'll be moving your lens almost

Used with quality gear and sound technique, a tele-converter (here, a 1.4x on a 300mm f/2.8) can achieve a little extra distance and help isolate a subject on the background.

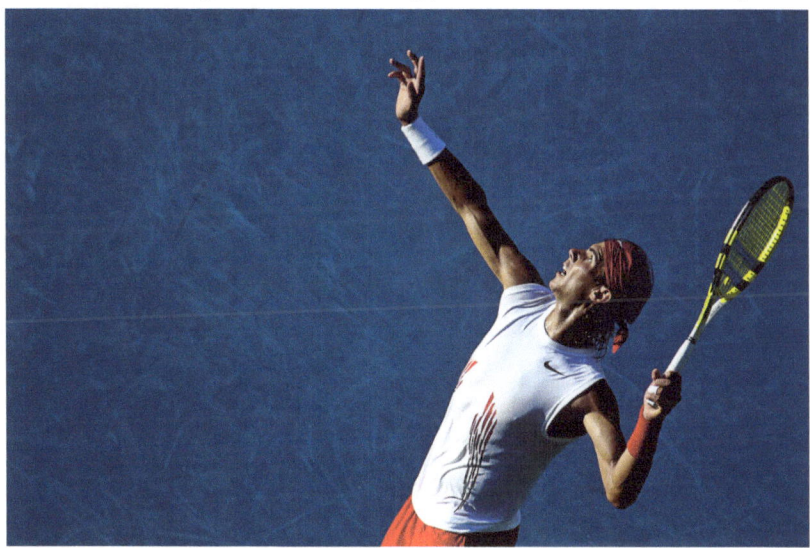

constantly while following a player around court.) The more magnification you use, the faster your shutter speed needs to be to prevent that blur from occurring. Consequently, using a teleconverter will require a faster shutter. For example, if you can usually shoot at 1/500 without incurring blur, adding a 1.4x may increase that minimum to as much as 1/1000. But that higher shutter speed is harder to attain now that the converter is cutting your light in half. (You can and should recover from this a bit by using a monopod, which we'll cover on page 31.)

Teleconverters also adversely affect autofocus in other ways. Even the very best give the lens and the camera's computer more to do, and the autofocus can become jumpy.

All these issues together combine to mean one thing: A converter won't make a bad lens good. In fact, it will make a good lens worse; more useful, perhaps, but definitely worse.

Does that mean you should avoid using teleconverters? Not necessarily. If you're using a fast, fixed-aperture, fixed-focal length, top-quality lens, and can work in strong light, and are using good support, and you can afford the best teleconverter with the most recent technology, then go ahead and add a 1.4x to your system. If you do, match brands with your lens, because the manufacturer optimized them to work together. Also, try not to use the combo at its widest aperture. And if you can't do all of this? Just move closer to your subject.

I carry a Nikon TC-14E—one of the best 1.4x converters ever made—but it hardly ever comes out of my bag. I use it only when no other solution will work.

Aperture

An important point to consider when buying lenses is their aperture potential.

First, you want lenses with large maximum apertures. The ideal is f/2.8, but you can certainly accomplish plenty with an f/4 lens. To give you an idea why, here's another statistic from my 2011 US Open work: I used an aperture of f/2.8 for 33 percent of my photos; I shot 55 percent at f/4. The remaining 12 percent of the photos were either scenic images or action compositions for which depth-of-field was more important than freezing motion. (For instance, I shot the action photo on the cover of this book at f/8 to keep everything from the court surface to the player's head in focus.)

When photographing tennis, as in photographing most sports, you often want to freeze the action. To do this in tennis, you need very high shutter speeds. And in order to achieve that, you need to either use a high ISO or shoot with a large aperture. The latter option is preferred, because the former will reduce your image quality.

In order to shoot at the required shutter speeds, even in bright sunlight you will most often need an aperture of at least f/4. If your lens has a maximum higher aperture, that doesn't mean you can't shoot tennis; it just means your exposure options will be limited. (Which, depending on how you view these kinds of things, is either an obstacle or an impetus to be creative.)

Second, try to avoid using zoom lenses with variable apertures (for example, f/4 at the low range of the lens and f/5.6 at the high end, such as a 70-300mm f/4-5.6). Lenses such as these almost never represent a brand's best glass, but that's not the primary reason for avoiding them. Using a lens like this means that as you zoom in and out while tracking a player around the court, your aperture

A wide-aperture lens enabled a 1/1600 at f/4 exposure to freeze the action.

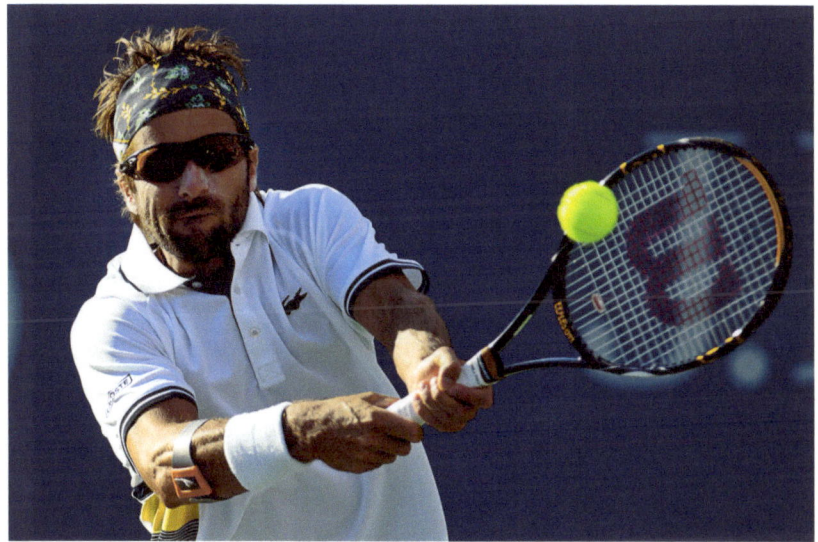

will change, and thus your exposure will change. As you'll read later in this book, I recommend setting your exposure manually, and obviously an oscillating aperture will impede that. Even if you ignore that suggestion and shoot in an automatic-exposure mode, then having a dynamic aperture will change either your depth of field or your shutter speed from frame to frame. The results will often be difficult to predict, and you'll end up with problems such as undesired focal planes and blurred players. You'll have an easier time photographing tennis with a fixed-aperture lens, such as a 70-200mm f/2.8, which maintains its f/2.8 aperture no matter how far you adjust its zoom.

If you *must* use a variable-aperture lens, then at least do so like this: Bypass manual exposure and use your camera in its Shutter Priority mode. This will ensure that you're freezing the action as you see fit. If you can control only depth of field *or* motion, in tennis photography you'll want the latter.

Lens Hoods

Most lenses come with hoods. Use them. If your lens did not come with a hood, or if you've misplaced the hood, buy a replacement. A hood will make two contributions to your tennis photography:

1. It will do the job it's built to do, which is to reduce lens flare when you aim your camera toward the sun (i.e., when you shoot back-lit).

2. Perhaps more importantly, the hood will protect your lens from physical damage. When photographing tennis, you'll often find yourself in close confines where you and your equipment can get bumped around a bit. Also, tennis players have been known to shank a ball now and then; errant shots can whack your gear pretty good. In a decade and a half of shooting tennis, I've been hit about two dozen times. A couple hoods have been dinged up, but I've never had a front element damaged.

Saving Hood Money

Replacement lens hoods can be expensive, especially for large telephotos. For example, the hood for my 300mm f/2.8 costs about $400. When it was permanently damaged a few years ago, I hesitated at replacing it at that price. In fact, I hesitated just long enough to save myself $390.

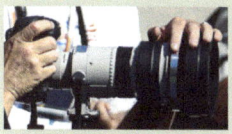 Fred Mullane, a friend of mine who's been shooting tennis twice as long as I have, found a cheaper and better solution: Go to your local hardware store and buy a 5-to 6-inch rubber drain coupling for about $10. The coupling will fit on the front of many 300mm f/2.8 lenses, though you may need to (carefully!) shave out a little of the rubber. Not only is this solution a big cost savings, but I actually like it better than the factory hood. Telephoto lenses can be cumbersome to carry. Hanging off your shoulder on long days, they tend to hit things, and I don't like $4,500 pieces of gear doing that. The rubber coupling is stiff, but with plenty of give that provides great shock protection.

If you're not partial to do-it-yourself solutions, you can also explore the camera world's third-party lens hoods. Most are less expensive than the camera manufacturers' versions, and some also offer added features (such as collapsibility).

CAMERA SUPPORT

My rule is that if a photo opportunity isn't good enough to warrant using something other than just my hand to support the camera, then the photo probably isn't good enough to shoot. Exceptions exist, but that rule serves me well. Even if a monopod or tripod isn't available (or cannot be used), you can gain extra support via other methods, such as bracing your elbow on your knee, or holding the camera against a hard surface. However, the best solution is to use the right tool for the job.

Monopods

If you use a lens that's 300mm or longer, use a monopod. In tennis, monopods are basic equipment. I always use one whether I'm shooting with a 600mm or a 300mm lens, and I've even occasionally used it with my 80-200mm.

Why? Part of the reason is to eliminate the risk of motion blur introduced by using long telephotos (as discussed in the previous section on teleconverters). When you're magnifying the frame that much, it's like using a lever on light: Even the slightest motion on your end can create a respectively drastic movement of your subject within the frame. Even when shooting at 1/800, a movement that is nearly imperceptible to you can blur your photo enough to turn it into a throw-away. A monopod helps prevent this, because it helps you keep the camera still. It will, in fact, allow you about two extra stops of stability. In other words, if you think you can effectively hand-hold a 300mm lens at shutter speed of 1/500, then a monopod will produce the same or better results at a shutter speed up to two stops lower (1/125).

The second reason for using a monopod is to combat fatigue. If you're spending a whole day shooting a tennis tournament, that long telephoto lens will feel heavier as the matches and hours pass. Using a monopod lets you rest that load even while you're working.

You do not, however, need to spend a lot of money on this. Many of the manufacturers craft excellent monopods with space-age materials. The leading raw material these days is super-light and super-strong carbon fiber (which, incidentally, is also used to make some of the best tennis racquets). While carbon fiber materials account for the best support gear in today's market, there's simply little need for a super-light monopod. After all, we're talking about just one post; this is support equipment made from the minimum of pieces. Even relatively heavy monopods don't weight enough to justify the price difference. For example, I have long used a Bogen 3218 monopod, which supports 26 pounds and weighs 1.7 pounds—and costs about $70. A very popular manufacturer's carbon-fiber monopod supports 26 pounds and weighs 1.1 pounds—and costs $230. So for nearly four times the price, you get nearly the exact same support performance at a savings of only half a pound.

If you're hiking through mountains and woodlands on a long back-country nature shoot, that half-pound could make a difference. (Of course, for that sort of shoot you'd probably be carrying a tripod, not a monopod.) But even

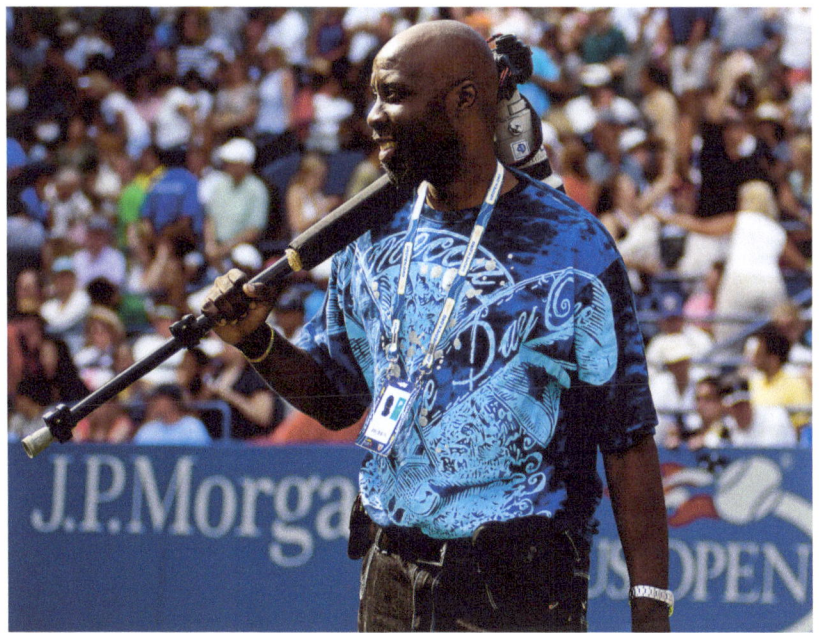

in the toughest tennis-photography conditions (say, shooting 30 matches in one afternoon at a Grand Slam event in 100-degree heat), your monopod will spend 99 percent of its day on the ground supporting your camera.

So no, you really don't need to buy a state-of-the-art monopod for photographing tennis. When choosing this gear, focus more on performance than lightness. Buy a monopod rated to support about twice the weight of the heaviest load you're likely to put on it. Make sure it has a rubber foot that won't slide and won't scrape a court surface. And make sure it has leg releases that you can unlock and lock quickly, and that won't slip. Another nice (but not critical) feature is a padded grip that will protect your hand from touching hot or cold metal (depending on the weather) and will help keep your hand from sliding even if you're perspiring.

You'll also need a head for your monopod. I recommend keeping this simple, too. You don't need a head that moves (such as a ball head), because nearly every time you use your monopod for tennis, you will likely be using a long lens with a built-in tripod collar that mostly serves the same purpose. Retailers and manufacturers will try to sell you on a head that just pans and tilts, but even those capabilities are

Holding a 300mm

Incidentally, you cannot effectively hand-hold a 300mm lens at a shutter speed of 1/500. If you don't believe me, run a test. Shoot some action photos (in real conditions) at 1/500 using just your hand for support, and some with a monopod. Enlarge the results on screen. Almost invariably you will see that your hand-held exposures will be a little blurrier. This effect will be exacerbated the longer into the day you shoot, as you fatigue.

This was true with film, but is even moreso true with digital, which renders motion blur more noticeably. The higher the resolution of the camera, the more blur will be apparent. And the smaller the sensor, the worse still. You can counteract this by using a lens with vibration-reduction technology, which generally boosts the lens cost by hundreds or thousands of dollars. Or you can use a $50 monopod.

If you're not concerned about a "little" motion, then consider this: Are you really okay with investing several thousand dollars (or even only several hundred) in camera gear just to create photos that are *almost* good, when you could improve them 400 percent by spending as little as an extra $30?

ancillary. In fact, I use a head that doesn't move at all. When photographing tennis, your panning can be accomplished by letting the entire monopod pivot on the ground, and there's not much need to tilt (though yes, tilting can be handy when shooting from a steep aerial angle). Any rotation you need is accomplished through the lens collar.

Whatever type of head you choose, just make sure it uses quick-release plates, which will allow you to rapidly swap lenses and bodies mid-match. I recommend using a head with an Arca-Swiss system, because the plates are interchangeable between the different manufacturers that have adopted the standard. Also, ensure that your monopod head uses plates that are compatible with any tripod head you may use. Then you never have to change plates, and any gear you own is always ready to be placed on any of your supports.

Tripods

You won't be using a tripod, at least not in a tournament environment, where it wouldn't even be allowed. If you're shooting in a private atmosphere, you could try using a tripod; but that amount of support is really unnecessary when photographing tennis. In fact, it would prove cumbersome and would restrict your mobility.

MEMORY

If I let myself reminisce, I begin to miss film. So I try not to think about it much. I try not to recall how easy it was to give the lab a dozen rolls of Velvia at the end of the day; meet some fellow photographers for dinner; pick up the processed slides the next morning; edit, sort and catalog them; then be back on court, refreshed and organized, shooting by 11 a.m. Now I spend dinner editing files, drink coffee to maintain a brisk working pace at 10 p.m.; get to bed late and hope to wake up early enough the next day to begin recycling through the process before the first match.

Lest I sound crotchety, allow me to mention that I do embrace new photo technology—perhaps even enthusiastically. Software such as Aperture and Adobe Lightroom have made the editing process relatively easy again; I love the instant gratification of digital; the immediate feedback on exposure and timing has become critical to the way I work; and I've grown irreversibly addicted to not thinking about the cost of film and processing when deciding whether to shoot a little extra.

Of course, all the wonders of the digital photography age rely on a key component: memory. All those millions of photo-bits need to be stored.

Cards

The primary storage target for your images is a memory card (unless you're shooting tethered to a laptop, a setup I can't recommend unless you're working for a client that needs instant access to your work, such as a wire service). Therefore, buy cards made by a manufacturer reputed for reliable products. (I use Lexar exclusively, because it's the first brand I bought and I've never had a problem that was the card's fault.)

Much ado is made about the ideal size for memory cards: too small and you'll have to load a blank card more often, too big and you'll risk losing a lot of work if the card fails. Until recently I still used 2-gigabyte (2GB) cards, because I invested in a bunch of them when they were the new standard. And I loved them. For a photographer who came into the business during the 36-shot film era, shooting over 100 frames before having to change media still felt luxurious. Also, because I use portable backup (see page 39), I was effectively unlimited in the amount of data I could record; using four small cards four times a day or two big cards once didn't make much difference to me. Either way, I can shoot continuously. (Now I use 8GB and 16GB.)

The more important factor in choosing cards is how fast they work with your camera. When photographing tennis, at times you'll be making so many exposures in quick succession that you'll be testing your camera's buffer. If you fill the buffer, the camera will stop letting you make new photos until the processor catches up. To avoid this problem, you want to use memory cards that your camera will be able to write to quickly. The faster the processor can write to the card, the faster it can free up buffer space, allowing you to keep shooting unimpeded by either end of your technology.

How fast do you need your cards' write speed to be? I recommend getting the fastest that work with your camera. (I would even get cards that can read faster than your camera can write, because then you'll be prepared for the next time you upgrade your gear.) However, when making this decision, don't rely solely on manufacturers' reports about how fast their cards are. I'm not suggesting that they're lying. The problem is that a particular card may work faster with one camera than with another. Research which cards work best with your gear (see the Appendix), look up how fast your camera can write data, and use that information to choose which cards to buy. (Incidentally, when a card is advertised as something like 300x, that's read speed, not write speed. Write is almost always slower.)

Another issue to consider is how many cards you need. This is affected primarily by the size of the cards (obviously you would need more 4GB cards than you would 64GB), and by your workflow. When I used 2GB cards, I rotated between four of them. I would dump each to a drive as soon as it came out of the camera, then re-format and use it again. Some photographers prefer to fill a card and then not touch it again until they have a chance to copy, back up and review all the images. For that tactic, bigger cards are mandatory.

WORKING WITH CARDS

Once you're on court, you'll quickly realize that you'll need a strategy for how to use your memory cards. The object is to avoid prematurely exhausting your available storage space. You do not want to back yourself into a position where a game, set or match is about to end and you have little or no room left on your current card. You also don't want to run out of memory in the middle of a point. If you do, I can tell you from experience that the player you're shooting will hit a diving volley or a between-the-legs shot at that exact moment.

Pay attention to how many files are on your card. You don't want to unexpectedly run out of room when a great moment happens in front of you.

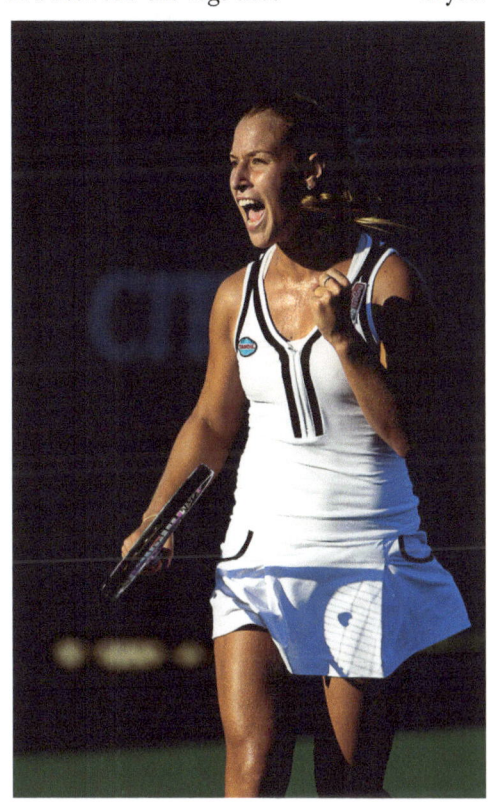

I try to avoid this situation by starting with this rule: Once I have fewer than a dozen frames of space left, I change to a new card the very next chance I get, which is usually after the current point ends. Why a dozen? Because I very rarely shoot more than 12 frames during one point; in modern tennis, points just don't last long enough for more than that. (If you find yourself shooting more frames than I, then just change your cutoff number to something that works better for you.) If you anticipate shooting a big game or a big point, then you'll probably want to change the card even sooner, just to be safe. You definitely want to have an empty card in the camera close to the end of a match, because you never know how many frames you'll need to record a post-match celebration, trophy presentation, etc.

Of course, changing cards takes time—not a lot, but enough to overlap with the next point if you're not quick about it. When I used to shoot film, I could change rolls in exactly the amount of time tennis players needed to get a new point started. Swapping cards takes just about as long. If you're new to shooting in tight spaces of time, you may want to practice changing your cards quickly, even when you're not in a rush. Often I'll plan for two points to change my card: After one point, I remove a new card from my carrying case; after the next point, I switch it with the full card.

My card-changing workflow also includes a data check. When I move my image files off a card and into permanent storage, I re-format the card immediately. When I swap cards mid-match, I always review the images before I start shooting again. If the camera shows me photos, I know I didn't dump that card; if the camera says the card is empty, then I know I can safely start shooting again. (Some photographers never re-format a card until home from a shoot. I've even met one photographer who never erases cards, but rather keeps each as a permanent archive. Only you can decide the strategy that makes you most comfortable.)

You want your cards to be able to record image data fast enough for you to shoot without pause—especially when capturing a burst of action or emotion.

Also, keep in mind that when you're shooting a match, it's easy to get lost in the photography and forget how many frames you have left on your card. Therefore, I recommend changing the way your camera alerts you to the frame count. Most cameras include a tally in the viewfinder, but often it shows how

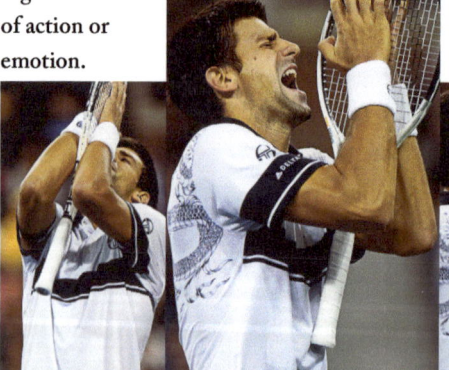
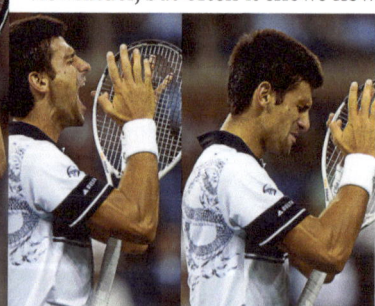

many frames *you have shot*. If your camera's custom functions allow it, have the display tell you how many frames are remaining instead. This way you'll always have that information in front of you without having to remove your eye from the viewfinder.

Backup

Although not mandatory, I advocate dumping cards while still on court, or at least having the means to do so. I didn't when I was first shooting digital, and I paid the price by accidentally re-using a card during an important shoot. The mistake cost me money and reputation with a client.

I now use a portable backup drive with a built-in card reader. Several good ones are available, but I use the Hyperdrive Colorspace. With this on my hip, I can remove a card from the camera and dump the data to the Colorspace's hard drive in just a few minutes. The data is automatically triple-checked, and then I'm free to re-format and re-use the card if needed. (However, I recommend not re-using a card unless necessary. You'll feel better knowing that you have your original copies of the files until you have a chance to move everything to permanent redundant storage later.)

This has become an integral part of my workflow, and I recommend it to every other photographer, regardless of whether you're shooting tennis, bocce, nature or whatever.

ANCILLARY GEAR

Of course, the photographer's bag contains more than just cameras and lenses and memory cards. But only some of what you might carry for other work is particularly useful when shooting sports.

Filters

I carry a polarizing filter when I'm photographing tennis, but I hardly ever use it. The only reason I carry one is that when it's needed, it's the only tool that will do the job. Even when I do use it, I do so almost exclusively for shooting ambiance—for example, photos of tournament grounds backed by a blue sky.

I *have* seen needs for a polarizing filter when shooting action. For instance, when working in some tennis stadiums the rails in the stands or the piping along the backscreens can produce glare at certain angles to the sun. That glare can present a distraction in the frame, ruining an otherwise solid photograph. A polarizer can help reduce that effect. Also, if you're shooting from a high angle, the sun can reflect off the court surface and wipe out some color. Using a polarizer can reduce that effect, too.

However, in most cases polarizing filters don't lend themselves well to tennis action photography, for two reasons:

This back-lit photo could have been better: A polarizing filter would have reduced the sunlight reflection on the court.

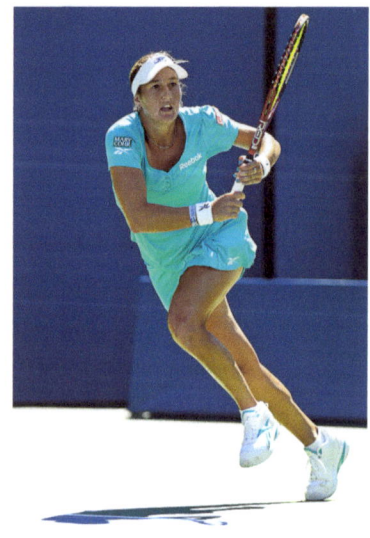

1. A polarizer absorbs one to two stops of light. Adequate light can be scarce in tennis photography, so you generally don't want to lose this much of it.

2. Since you'll be using autofocus, you'll need a circular polarizer, which needs to be rotated to adjust it to the desired strength. Once you've set the filter, if you quickly rotate the camera 90 degrees during a point (to switch between horizontal and vertical), you will lose your polarization, negating the effect. And because you had to change your exposure by one or two stops to compensate for the light loss caused by the filter, you will now also be overexposing your photos. If you're using a lens with an external filter, you can try to hold the polarizer while rotating the camera, thereby keeping the polarizing effect. However, that's harder in practice than in theory during a fast tennis point. Moreover, if you're shooting with big glass, your filter will be *inside* the lens, operable by a small external dial. Then you'll have two motions to complete in the middle of a point, when it's nearly impossible to accomplish one.

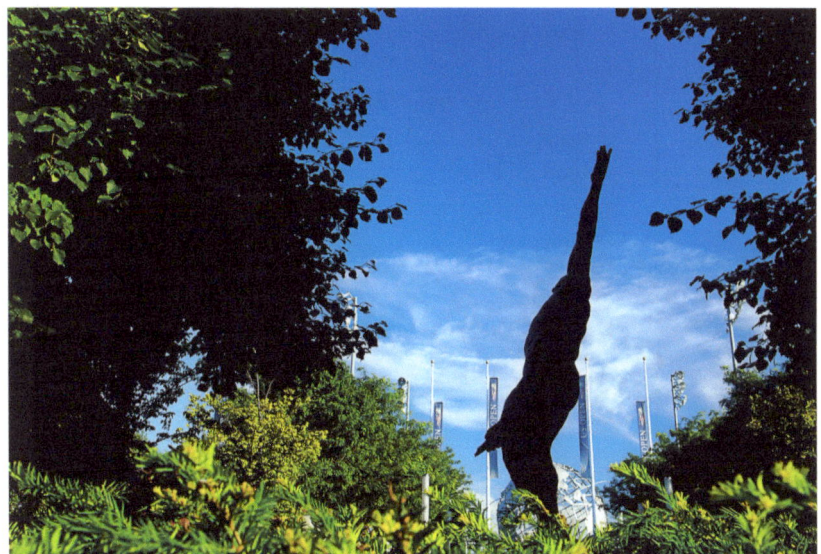

I've also tried using warming filters to improve the quality of harsh light, but the effect usually looked artificial. They can be a useful tool when shooting a nature scene full of rich, warm colors; tennis scenes, however, tend to be filled with cool colors that end up just looking yellowed when warmed with a filter.

Besides, nowadays warming filters are nearly obsolete. Using any of the myriad image-editing software applications on the market, you can add warmth to the tone of a photo with just a click or two of a mouse. Moreover, you can use computer technology to adjust or correct white balance much more easily and accurately than you ever could have using filters and color meters with film.

One type of filter to consider using is a UV, not for optical effect, but to protect the front element of your lens. This is a common technique, but one I don't use. What exactly would I be protecting my lens against? In tennis, I admit to the possibility of a ball hitting the front element. But I've already advised using a lens hood; the chances are slim that a ball could avoid the hood but still strike the glass. In over 15 years of shooting, this has never happened to me, nor have I seen it happen to anyone else. Using a UV filter as lens protection merely introduces another layer of glass between you and your subject — one more layer of glass

A polarizing filter can make the sky appear more blue by removing reflections from moisture droplets in the atmosphere, and foliage more green by reducing glare on shiny leaves.

to keep clean, and, moreover, a flat layer of glass that will increase your probability of lens flare.

As for any other filters you may own (split neutral-density, for example), leave them home. They have no place in tennis. (That is, of course, unless you're planning on making ambiance photos—then all creative tools are eligible for duty.)

Bags & Such

All this camera gear I've recommended needs to somehow be carried. There's not much advice I can offer in this area other than to use whatever you're comfortable working with and out of.

Some people love shoulder bags, because they're easy to carry, put down and flip open. Other people prefer a hip-bag, because it doesn't need to be carried or put down, and it's also easy to open. Other people prefer a backpack-style bag (despite it not being easy to put down and open) because its load is ergonomically distributed, resulting in fewer sore muscles. Others don't carry any bag; they just tote the camera(s) mounted with the lens(es) they think they'll want to use.

My strategy is a hybrid of some of the above. When photographing tennis, I usually carry one body mounted with a long telephoto lens that's attached to a monopod. I carry this with the lens' strap over my shoulder so that the camera and lens hang next to my hip, with the monopod pointed upward alongside my torso. (Note that I put the *lens'* strap on my shoulder, not the camera's. You don't want big glass hanging off the front of a camera body without being supported, or you could damage the lens mount.) I tighten the tripod collar lock so the monopod won't fall. I keep my hand either on the monopod or under the lens, just in case the strap breaks or comes undone (an unlikely event, but one that would be disastrous to the gear if it occurred). I also wear a small hip-bag, where I stow a shorter lens (usually an 80-200mm f/2.8), spare memory cards, Hyperdrive, teleconverter, polarizing filter, business cards, notebook, pen and a few Twizzlers. (The Twizzlers are a snack. They serve no photographic purpose.) If I feel I need to carry a third lens (say, a wide-angle zoom), I attach a lens belt-case to the pack's strap, right next to my water-bottle holster. This setup keeps one hand free and my shoulders relatively free of burden.

I do not wear a photo vest on court. I did in the past, but tennis photography almost always happens on hot, sunny days—conditions inconducive to extra layers of clothing.

I have thought about trying a belt system, such as the one made by Tamrac. They're designed ergonomically and allow you to attach cases that match the size of different lenses and accessories. A more snug fit is a more secure fit. (Despite using a hip-bag, I'm not crazy about how a lens can flop around inside—or how it can fall out if you neglect to zip the top closed. I learned this lesson the expensive way.) If you want to try a belt system, I recommend using the attachments that close via zipper, not Velcro; the latter is so strong that it's too loud to open during tennis.

LIMITATIONS FOR FANS

One last note about camera equipment is to make sure you'll be allowed to use it.

If you're at a tour event with or without a credential, the only gear you may be hassled about is a video camera. Tournaments make most of their money from television rights, and whoever has paid for those rights wants to have control over all video production at the event. Other than that, you can probably expect to be allowed to shoot with any camera and lens, as long as it doesn't interfere with play. (For instance, extreme rapid-fire cameras used to photograph detailed sequences tend to be pretty loud. To use them, a photographer needs to insulate the sound with a blimp, shoot from far away, or both.)

If you're a fan or parent bringing your camera to a regulated event, you may have limitations imposed on you. Many professional sporting events limit the size of bags you may

Some tournaments limit how large your gear can be if you don't have a press credential.

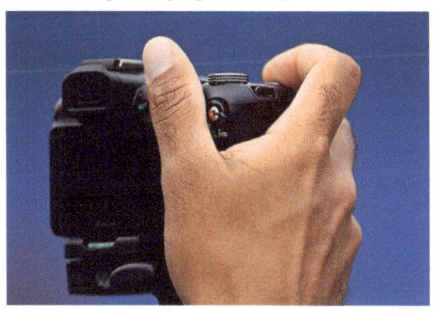

carry onto the grounds. Also, some tournaments simply don't want unauthorized media covering their events; to ensure this, they limit the camera gear that fans can use. For instance, the Australian Open has a rule barring spectators from carrying a lens longer than 200mm. (Of course, a teleconverter or a 1.5x sensor can help you get around this restriction a bit.)

In most cases you'll be okay. I just recommend checking for potential restrictions before you arrive.

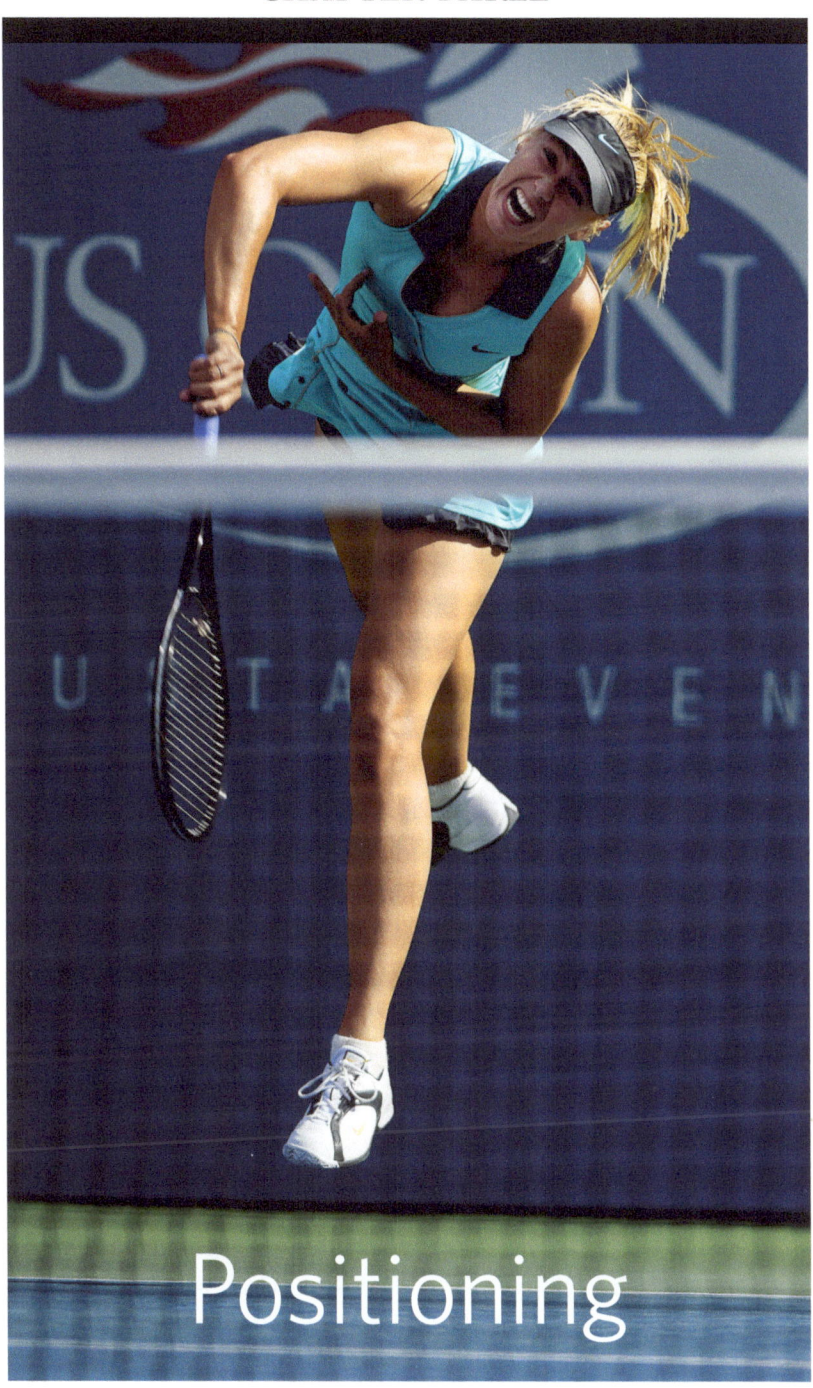

CHAPTER THREE

Positioning

POSITIONING

In tennis, you never really know where a defining moment will happen. You can guess; you can narrow the options a bit (for instance, a winning player will usually turn toward family or friends in the stands); but you really never know for sure what will happen and where. You could move to what you think is a perfect angle only to see the perfect photo opportunity develop in the spot you just left. Experience has taught me that the best photo will usually happen where I was last seated. That's not meant as a cynical observation, but rather a statistical one; the longer you stick with an idea, the closer you'll be to it working out.

Of course, you have to move sometimes. You can't sit in the same seat, or stand in the same spot, for an entire day. All your photos would end up looking similar. But the first trick, before staying put (for a little while), is to know where to position yourself in the first place.

As discussed in Chapter 1, you will be limited to where you can shoot from, either by tournament rules, by etiquette or by courtesy. These limitations are the first thing to know, and then you can pick your spot from what space remains.

When you arrive at a court, look at the light conditions, look at what the players are wearing, look at the backgrounds. You first need to know how you have to shoot, and second how you like to shoot. Consider the angle of the light. Consider the type of photos you want to make (tight action? wide angle? running? serving?). If at a competetive event, consider where the players' family/friends/coaches are sitting (you can often find this by watching players' reactions during the match). Survey your options, then pick among them. Then, if you change your mind, wait until the next changeover before moving.

COMMON ANGLES

If you're shooting strokes—forehands, backhands, serves, volleys—then you'll need to choose an angle that will allow for the best results. You can't sit or stand just anywhere and expect the photos to look great.

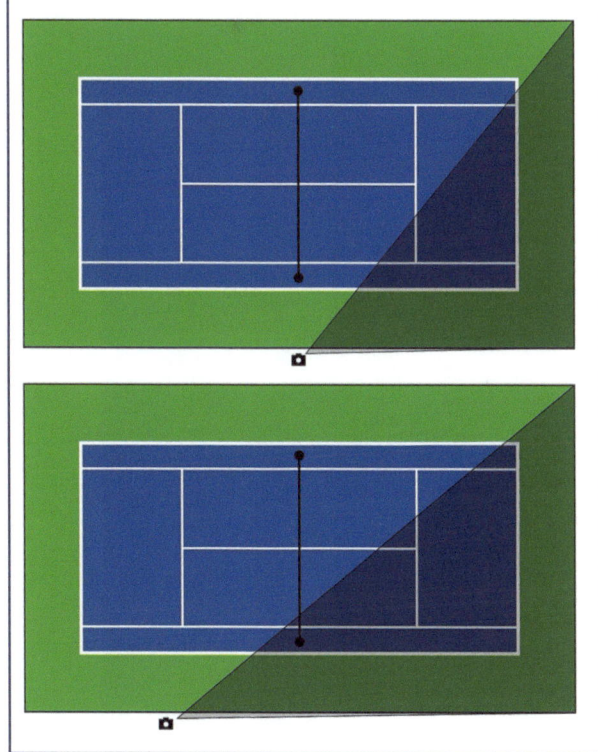

Figure 3

From a sideline position at the center of the court, you can shoot toward just about any spot you could expect a player to be. However, this may restrict your options more than you'd like. For example, if you want to use the backscreen as a uniform background, the shaded area is where you could aim to make that happen (top). But it's a small percentage of the area of play. By moving back toward the opposite service line (bottom), you can see how much more of the playing area falls into your camera's range.

Many people new to tennis photography assume that the best position is at the center of the side of the court, even with the net, so that you have equal visual access to both players. The obvious advantage to this is that from your point of view, you could shoot almost anything that happens anywhere on court. That's why photographers from newspapers and wire services like to sit there — no matter where some big moment happens, they will probably be able to photograph it from that spot.

However, though the center of the sideline can be good for providing total coverage, it's not always the best spot for the best photography (see Figure 3). Consider the fact that the most expensive seats in a tennis stadium are usually at the ends of the court, not the sides, and that the television cameras are also positioned behind the baseline.

Also consider the fact that shooting from the center angle forces you into some aesthetic situations you might not prefer. (For example, when the player hits a wide ball,

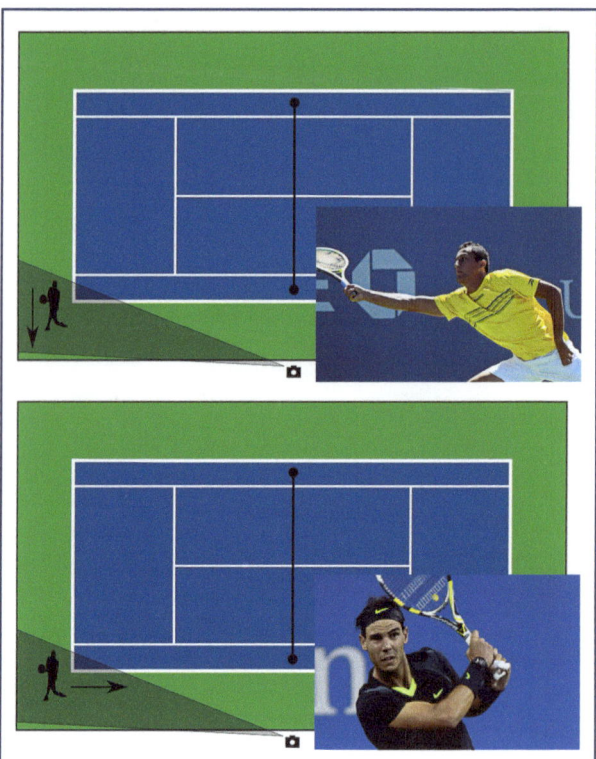

Figure 4
Sitting at the middle of the sideline allows for a nice angle for some photos, but presents a problem for making others. For instance, if the player runs wide to hit a forehand, you'll be aiming almost straight down the line and he or she will be looking as much as 90 degrees away from the camera (top). However, you could get a nice photo on the follow-through, when the player will be looking more in your direction (bottom). This is an example of why knowing what type of photo you want to make is important to choosing a shooting position.

his or her eyes will almost always be looking away from the camera. See Figure 4.) It can also present you with some physical obstacles, which we'll explore soon.

I'm not suggesting that you should never shoot from the center, just that it might not be your favorite spot if you know what you can do from elsewhere. (Even if you decide you love shooting from the center of the court, you probably won't want to shoot *only* from there.)

Let's assume you want to shoot ground strokes hit from the baseline—which account for a majority of the shots in a match. Among your first considerations is whether you want to be shooting forehands or backhands. This will dictate which side of the court you shoot on. You probably don't want the player to be moving away from the camera during the shot, so you'll need to pick the side of the court where he or she will be moving toward you on that stroke (see Figure 5). The same is true if you want to photograph the serve. And your angle for shooting either will also be

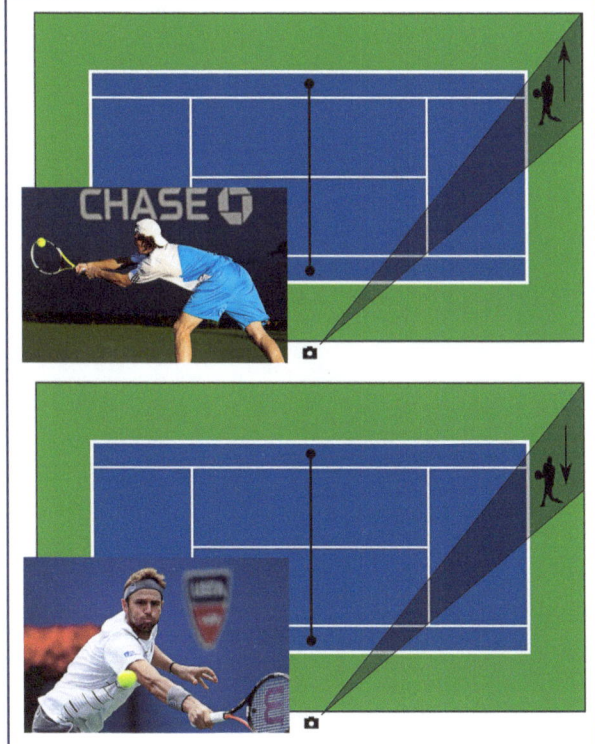

Figure 5
Generally you want to shoot the player hitting on the side closer to you, to avoid getting photos of him or her moving and looking away from the camera (top). You can also think of this as keeping the ball between you and the player. From this position and angle, a better photo is possible by waiting for a ball up the middle, when the player is facing me (bottom).

affected by whether the player hits right- or left-handed. After that, the decision can get even more involved. It's not enough to know which side of the court to be on—you also have to decide where on that side of the court to be.

AN ANGLE EXPERIMENT

Just as an exercise, experiment with shooting a player hitting a certain stroke from different angles and at different points in their swing. You'll find that the player looks better from some spots than from others, and at different instants of his or her swing motion. For example, a player will usually look a little awkward at the instant between hitting the ball and following through with the racquet—lanky, perhaps, with the racquet held out at a weird angle, protruding from the rest of the frame with no purpose in the composition. The player can look good before that instant and after, but not usually between.

As with any type of photography, your angle (combined

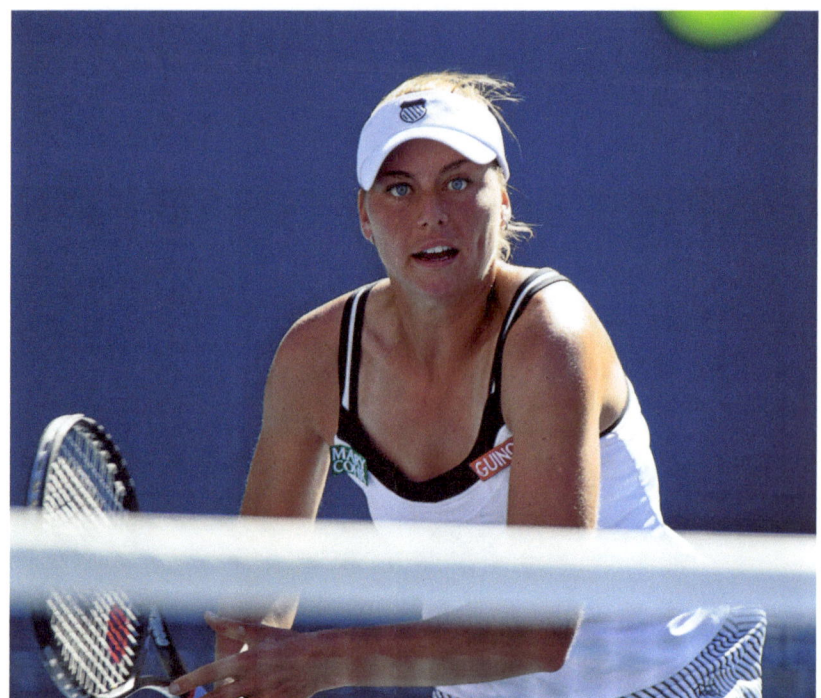

Action photos
tend to be more
dynamic when the
player is looking
toward (or even at)
the camera.

with lens choice) will often force your composition; at the
very least it will eliminate some compositional options. In
tennis, if your angle has backed you into a composition
that's possible only in that instant between contact and
follow-through, then your photos won't look that great. So
you'll find that you need to choose an angle that allows for
the best compositions at more photogenic moments of the
player's stroke.

In this experiment, you'll also find that it's impossible to
include the ball in a compositionally pleasing way from some
angles, and that it's impossible to include it at all from other
angles. Let's assume you're trying to compose a tight action
photo of a backhand, with the ball in the frame. There's only
a fraction of a second when the ball will be close enough to
the player so that you can frame them simultaneously. Also
consider that when a player hits the ball, his or her arms are
extended out from the body; if you're framing tightly from
too wide an angle, you won't be able to include the player's
face, arms and racquet in the same photo, let alone the ball.
You therefore need to be shooting from an angle that will

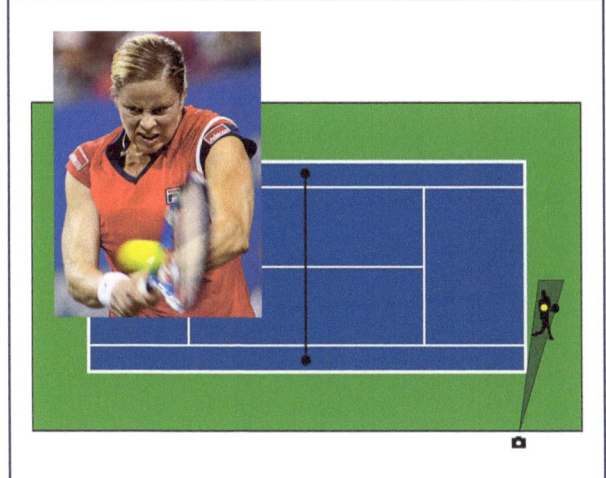

Figure 6
If you want to shoot the ball at a particular moment in the player's swing, then determine how to align your camera with the ball and the player at that moment.

array the ball, the racquet and the player's face all within a narrow visual corridor extending from your lens (see Figure 6). The same is true for a forehand, a volley, an overhead, a serve, and so on. Just as every stroke is hit differently, every stroke requires a slightly different nuance to photograph it well. (More on this in Chapter 7.)

ALTERNATIVE ANGLES

So far the positions we've covered are the most common ones, the ones along courtside, the ones from which most tennis photos you'll want to make are made. But they're not the only positions, they're not the only angles.

Your options are limited only by your creativity—and, of course, by rules and etiquette.

Backcourt

A great angle for capturing dynamic action is from behind the backcourt. In fact, this is perhaps my favorite angle to shoot from. With a long telephoto lens, you can photograph the player at the far end of the court while using the net as an out-of-focus foreground element that lends a sense of place. Because the player will almost always be facing you after he or she hits the ball, you can get some very dynamic follow-through photos. And if you wait, you can get the ball in those images, too. When the shot is coming right toward you, the ball gets larger and out of focus (see the photo on page 56), which can lead you into some great and uncommon compositions.

Also, from this same angle you can use a wide-angle lens to photograph the player on the close end of the court. Many creative options are available with this setup, such as framing a server against the background crowd, or capturing a player running down a wide shot in the corner.

Unfortunately you usually can't shoot pros from this spot. If you're credentialed at a professional tournament, you will sometimes find official photographer positions behind the baseline. A few big tournaments have windows in the backscreen for this purpose, or even a spot in the corner behind some signage.

But at most pro events, your best chance of shooting from this angle is by getting into the stands. If you're credentialed, this isn't always allowed, so you might actually be better able to access this position as a ticket-holder. Another option is that if you attend the early rounds of a tournament, you may be able to find empty general seating behind the baseline on the side courts. (Incidentally, the side courts

The backcourt provides ample opportunities for shooting with a wide-angle lens. Among other possibilities, you can get both players framed in the same photo.

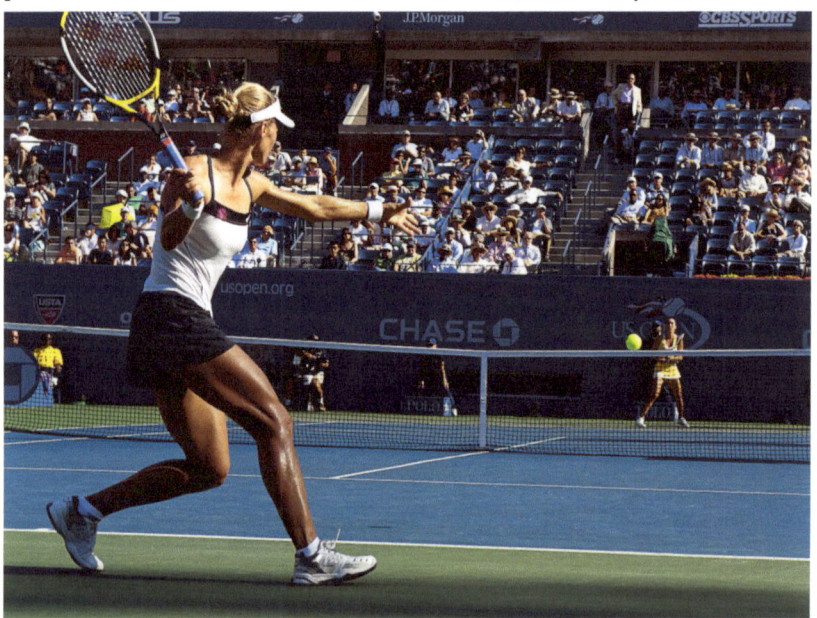

at a professional tournament are the best place for ticket holders to shoot action photos of pro tennis players. It's the one place where you can sometimes get as close to the action as credentialed photographers can.)

At amateur tournaments, you may find backcourt access even more difficult. You won't find windows in the screen, and you probably won't find backcourt seats. You won't be allowed to sit in that spot *on* the court, and you probably wouldn't want to anyway because you'd get hit with a ball—several times, most likely. If there's no windscreen, you could try standing just outside the court and shooting through the fence; using a wide aperture should throw the fence enough out of the depth of field so that it's rendered invisible in your image. To have a chance of this working, you will need to stand as close to the court as possible, almost to the point of your lens touching the fence.

Shooting from behind the court (when allowed or appropriate) is a great angle for getting the ball in the photo along with eye contact from the player.

Aerial

Another great angle (that's also hard to find) is shooting from above the court. A few tournaments (such as the Australian Open) allow photographers to work from catwalks above the main stadium. But to qualify for that access, you need to have a credential and a sizeable amount of liability insurance. Alternatively, try to find spots in the top seating tiers of tennis stadiums, where you can shoot down on the court; if you can get all the way up to the last row, you might even be able to shoot down on adjoining side courts.

Keep in mind that you don't necessarily need to achieve altitude. Because the slope of a stadium is usually uniform, getting higher doesn't change your angle, it just increases

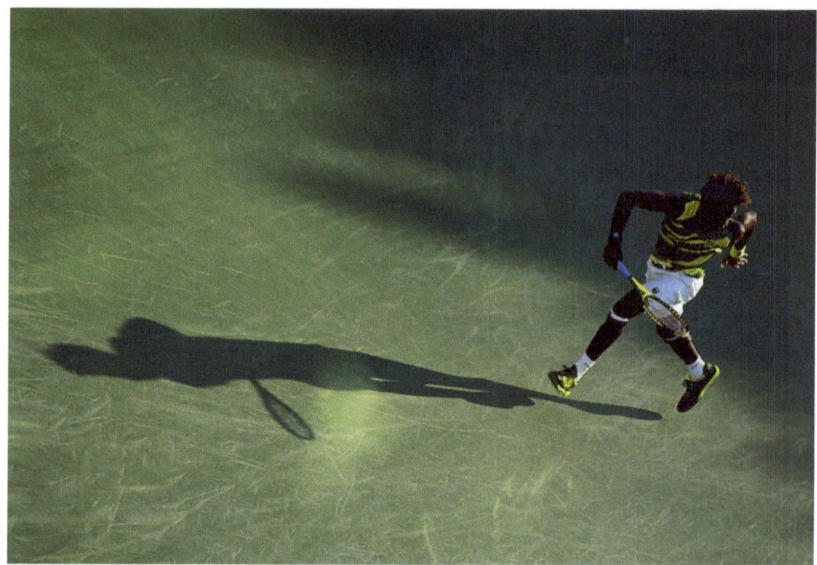

Toward the end of the day, shooting from up top will allow you to use warm light and long shadows in a way not possible from ground level.

your need for a longer lens. You want to be high enough so that you can use a long enough lens to eliminate distracting background elements from your photo, but not so high that you need an 800mm to find the player on court.

From these high angles you can be incredibly creative, as the position offers some advantages:

- You can shoot from an angle that most viewers will not have frequently seen, which automatically makes your images look different than 99 percent of others.

- You'll also be shooting from non-eye level, which is generally eye-catching, as it provides a view away from the norm of how people usually see (which can often make any photo better).

- You have excellent control over keeping clean backgrounds, because you can use the court surface as a backdrop.

- You can use the court markings (lines and colors, for example) as interesting compositional elements.

- In bright sunlight, you get great shadows that you can use to make creative compositions.

- Midday light can be easier to work with from up high. At ground level, noon light is unflattering top light, but from a 45-degree aerial angle, it's side light. (More on this in Chapter 5.)

With these advantages come challenges. The higher your shooting position, the longer lens you'll need to reach the court, or the more creative you'll have to be with shorter lenses (such as including the crowd in your composition). You also may have to deal with the sun reflecting off the court, which can drastically alter what you may be expecting as a proper exposure. Additionally, that sun can cause glare on the ground, washing out your color (introducing a good use for a polarizing filter).

Also, you may want to use a smaller aperture than usual. When photographing shadows, remember that they become part of the composition, part of the subject. Therefore, you may want them to be in focus along with the player. An aperture of f/4 will probably not achieve that goal; instead, try to shoot at f/5.6 or f/8.

Another challenge is more of a creative one. Try to avoid the trap of thinking that just because you're working from an unusual angle, that that's enough to make your photos good. You still need to apply all the rules of composition and all the criteria you normally would to your image-making deci-

Shooting from a high angle can be great at midday, because you can use those harsh shadows as a compositional element.

sions. Don't settle for the hum-drum moment, just as you wouldn't settle for it from courtside; look for dynamic moments that show energy or excitement or emotion. Also, remember that a dramatic shadow doesn't make a good photo by itself; that shadow needs to be used in an aesthetically

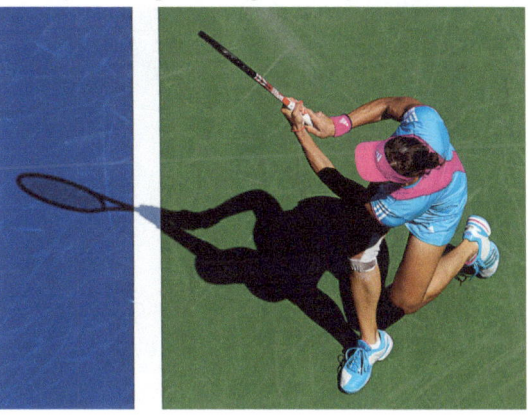

pleasing way. And you probably want to avoid cutting off a player's shadow at the edge of the frame, just as you would avoid cropping a player's body in an awkward place (see page 92).

BACKGROUNDS

A clean or controlled background (left) makes for a better photo than a background filled with a chaos of random distractions (right).

The single most overlooked issue in creating quality photographs in any niche is the background. Neglecting it is a sin committed almost always by the beginner, often by the intermediate, and sometimes even by the advanced photographer. Controlling the background is so critical to making good images that once a developing photographer internalizes the concept, his or her work immediately improves immensely. A good background is often the difference between an acceptable photo and a great one.

This is a truism in sports photography, too, except the learning curve is even steeper. Even photographers who know to control the background in a portrait or nature scene often forget to do so when shooting sports. The reason is twofold. First, much

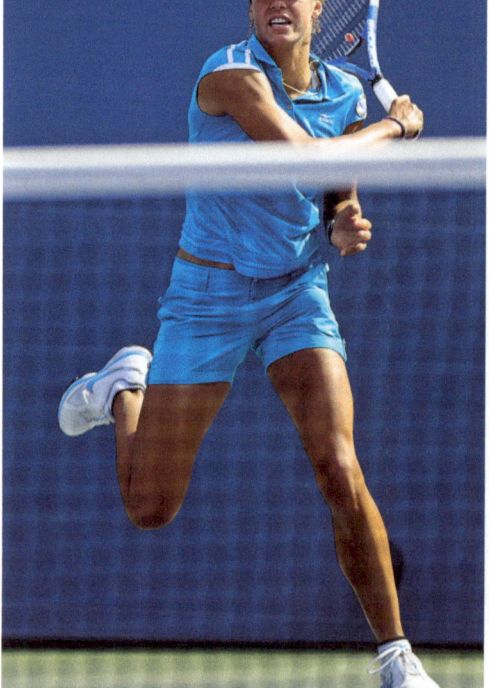

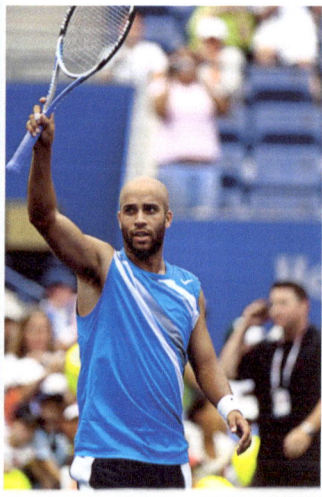

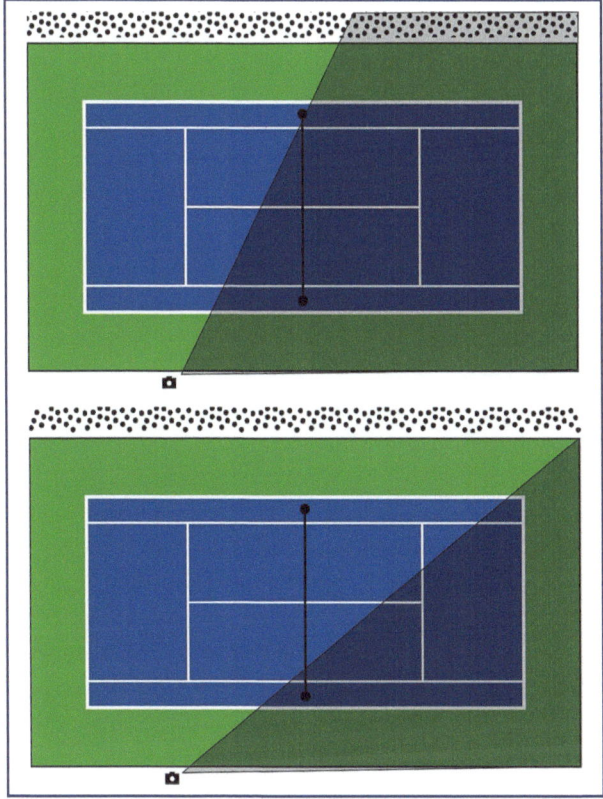

Figure 7
Backgrounds at the sides of the court (whether at organized tournaments or in casual settings) can be filled with visual noise, such as a crowd or other courts. If you aren't concerned about that noise, or if you can control it, you have a wide window to shoot in (top). Most events (and even some public courts) provide a great solution: You can often use the backscreen as a nice, uniform background. However, the price is a narrower angle of court coverage (bottom).

of sports photography is following the game, watching the ball, tracking the player, waiting with an itchy shutter finger for an exact moment of compelling competition to happen in front of the lens. In the midst of that, it's easy to forget about the background. Second, when you're doing all of that following and watching and tracking and waiting, in an environment you can't control, in which you can't even move, managing the background is hard. Considering all of this, some tennis photographers don't even think of trying to control the background; some others just don't bother.

Because you have less control over your background once you choose a position to shoot from, you need to consider your background carefully *before* choosing your spot. You'll want to consider several criteria, including the location of light and shadows, whether a player is right- or left-handed, what strokes you'll be shooting and where the ball will likely be when the player hits it. (I'm not suggesting this is easy.

It's anadvanced concept to master. But I promise that it's a goal worth working toward.)

The first point to consider is whether the sides of the court will provide an acceptable background. In an amateur setting, they usually won't. Whether in a public park or at a club, tennis courts are usually grouped close together. At the side of one court is another court, followed by another, sometimes by even another and another past that. So if you shoot toward the side of your court, your background becomes a mess of other nets, neighboring players, trash cans, net posts, meandering balls, benches, bags and kids on seesaws behind the chain-link fence.

In a professional tennis setting, shooting toward the side of the court becomes a little more practical, because it's generally filled with spectators that you can uniformly blur by using a wide aperture. Still, the sidelines of a pro court can introduce other problems, such as shiny railings in the box seats, courtside security personnel in bright shirts, or the changeover chairs that are often a mess of strewn towels, stray clothes and spare racquets.

Shadow, shallow depth of field and creative use of light can make for a great background — and can even obscure otherwise unwanted background distractions.

In many cases — in professional and amateur tennis environments — you'll find that your cleanest backgrounds will be along the backscreens. Therefore, if you limit your backgrounds to the backcourt, you will often improve your photos.

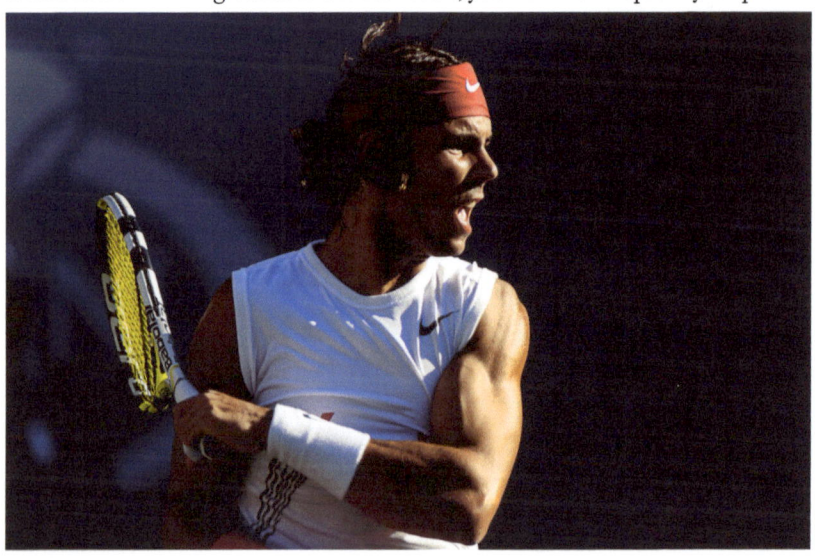

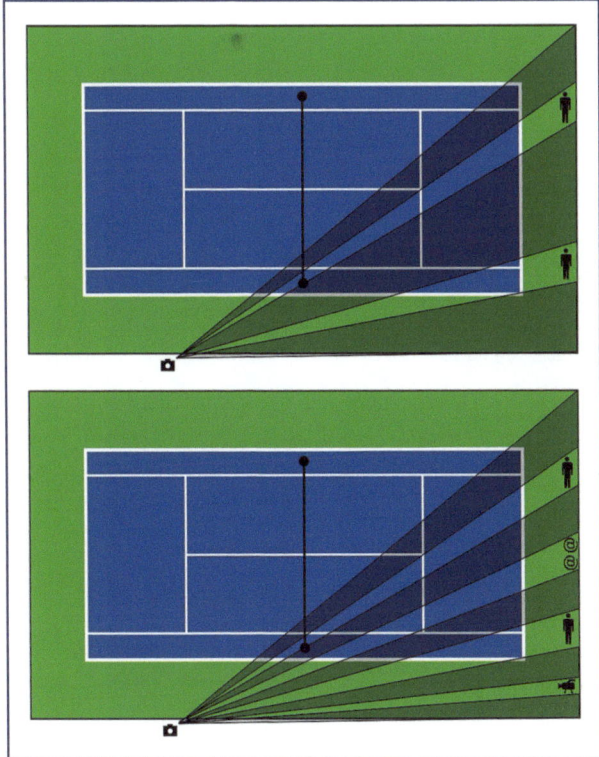

Figure 8
Obtaining a uni-
form background
can be difficult.
Here, two line
umpires (at an
organized event)
fragment your
angle. Avoid-
ing them in your
frame splits your
court coverage into
three pieces (top).
For more trouble,
add a television
camera and a big
tournament logo
on the backscreen
(bottom). If you
avoid all of them,
you can see how
limited your court
coverage becomes.
Instead of one big
window to shoot
in, you're reduced
to several narrow
windows, all just
to allow for a clean
background in your
photographs. You'll
have fewer image-
making opportuni-
ties, but the photos
you do make will
look more polished.

However, there are downsides to this. First, you will halve your court coverage (see Figure 7). Second, if photographing an organized tournament, you'll likely face three more challenges in the on-court background: logos, officials (line umpires and ballkids) and sometimes television cameras. As with many artistic choices, whether to include or exclude these elements in the background is a question that different photographers will have different answers to. Some feel that these elements are natural to the tennis environment, and therefore it's natural to see them in the background; they may even argue that the logos, officials and television cameras help provide a sense of place. Other photographers feel that any recognizable element aside from the player and the action detracts from the quality of the photo.

I can also tell you this: Some of the first group believe what they do because achieving what the second group believes is not easy. Excluding logos, officials and television cameras from tournament-tennis photos can sometimes

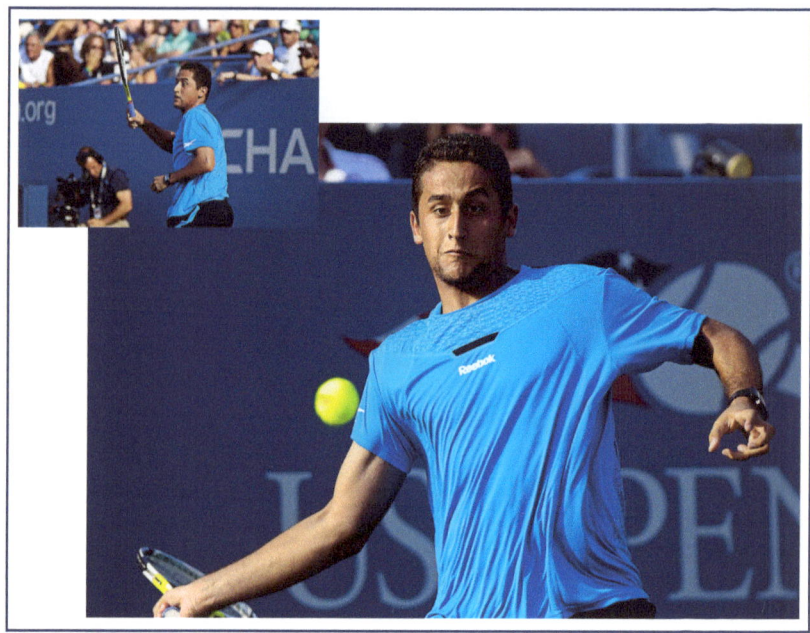

Figure 9

If you find you just can't keep distractions such as television cameras and too much crowd out of your backgrounds (inset), you can try using a longer lens from a different angle to help isolate your subject better.

be so hard that it seems impossible. The problem is that eliminating these elements fragments your viewing angles, leaving you with little court coverage, just narrow slices of usable space where you hope some action will happen (see Figure 8).

A simple solution is to shoot with a telephoto lens. Telephotos focus in on a very narrow angle, which allows you to better isolate some elements of a scene from others. You'll find that moving your position by even a few inches can dramatically alter your angle of view.

Switching to a longer lens will also, of course, force you to frame your photos tighter. You can use that fact creatively, or you can pick a different position to increase the distance between you and the player (see Figure 9).

The Payoff

The natural question is whether the result is worth all this effort. Can you imagine abandoning what would have been a good action photo just because a line umpire was mucking up the background? Can you throw away an opportunity for the sake of quality?

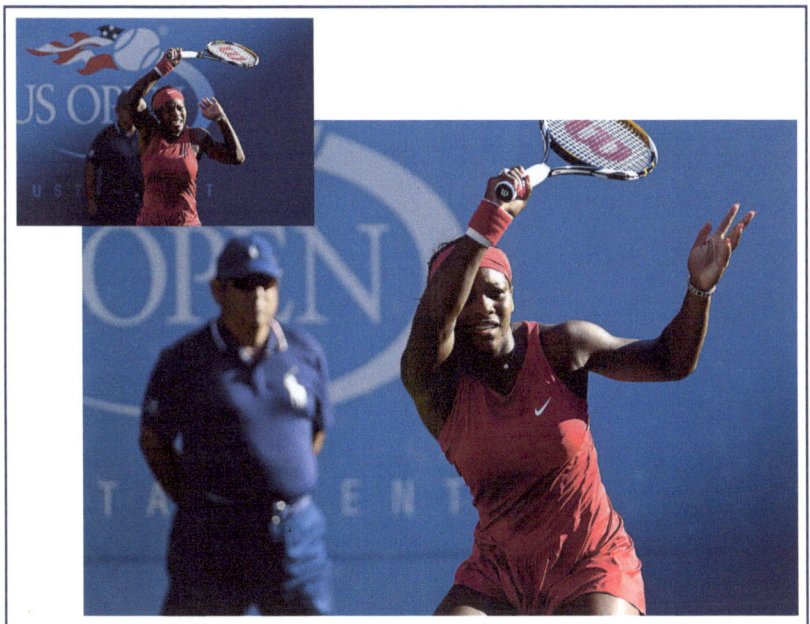

The answer depends on your goal. Do you want to make more images that are just satisfactory, or fewer images that are better? Perhaps you need a lot of photos just for demonstration purposes, or maybe you need only one photo that's good enough to license for magazine use. You need to choose your artistic preferences, and you need to decide what your photographic priorities are—what are your criteria for how clean your images need to be?

My preference about these background elements is relatively strict, but not entirely. I try to keep my backgrounds as clean as I can, even if it means abandoning good moments of action. However, notice I say "good," not "great." I've sometimes sat through a whole game without shooting one frame because all I was presented with was routine backhands in front of bad backgrounds. But if I'm shooting Roger Federer about to hit a between-the-legs shot in a Grand Slam final, I open the shutter regardless of whether a TV camera is sticking out of his back. Sometimes story is more important than composition.

In other words, circumstance matters. The specifics of the moment are an important criterion. (How do you know the impending action will be good enough to compensate

Figure 10
Court officials don't always ruin the background of a photo. Just be careful that they don't converge with your main subject (inset). Carefully placed in the frame, they can even add to the story of the photo or help balance the composition.

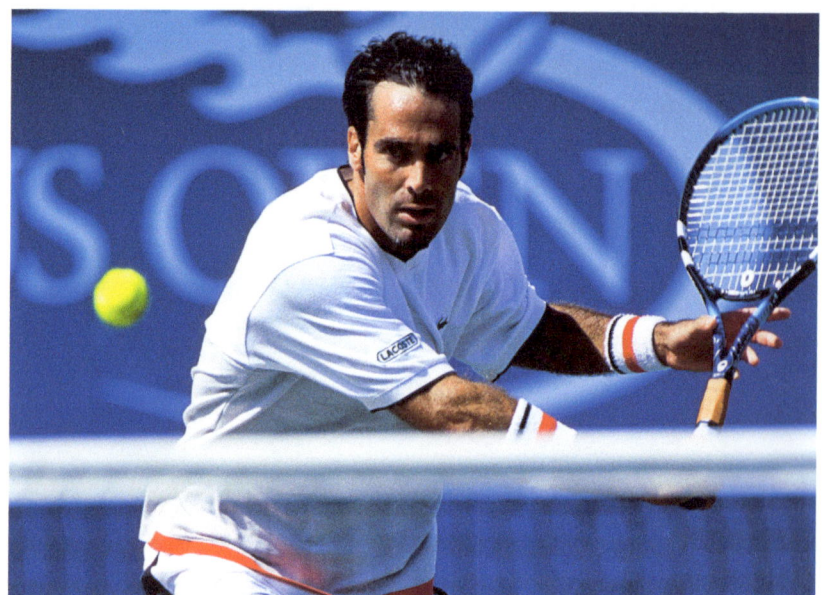

Background logos aren't always bad in a photo. For example, a tournament logo can add a sense of place, a sense of importance to the moment captured.

for a bad background? Sometimes you don't. That's why it's okay to just shoot anyway and throw out the junk later.)

Outside of those special moments, I prefer to keep the background uncluttered. I like to keep the sponsor logos out, the officials out, the cameras out. That's hard to do, but the clean backgrounds make the photos look better—they keep the viewer's eyes solely on the player and the action.

Still, I appreciate that these background elements can add a sense of place. Sometimes they add it in a marketable way; as much as I prefer photos that don't have a tournament logo in the background, the tournament organizers love them. The same goes for sponsors and their logos.

Also, having a line umpire in the background helps put the tennis player in a competitive context (see Figure 10), and if that official is signaling a call, that can even help tell a story in the photo. Likewise, an on-court television camera in the background may tell the viewer that this moment of action happened in an important match, and a tournament logo can indicate that the match is important.

So yes, you can effectively allow these elements into your photos. But—and here's the important caveat—you should do so only when they help the photo, and never when they detract. If that umpire is only half visible behind the player's back, then that's breaking an important rule of composition; that's convergence. If that television camera's lens is glaring in the sun, then that's breaking another important rule of composition; that's the point of highest contrast falling outside of your main subject.

Yes, this makes photographing tennis more difficult. But it also makes your photos better, which, no matter why you're shooting, is always more rewarding.

OBSTACLES

Almost as challenging as avoiding unwanted elements behind the action is working around obstacles in front of it. In tournament matches, almost anywhere you position yourself will put some potential obstacle between you and part of the tennis.

If you sit near center court on one side, you may have change-over chairs or an umpire chair blocking part of your view. The same position on the other side of the court (at a pro event) can put TV cameras in front of you, and any position that helps you avoid them can put ballkids in front of you. Trying the backcourt can put line umpires in front of you, and getting into the stands can put spectators in front of you. All of this gets worse as a tournament nears its finale, because more officials and more TV cameras are added for the more important matches.

What's a tennis photographer to do? Work around them. As you'll remember from the "Code of Conduct" discussion

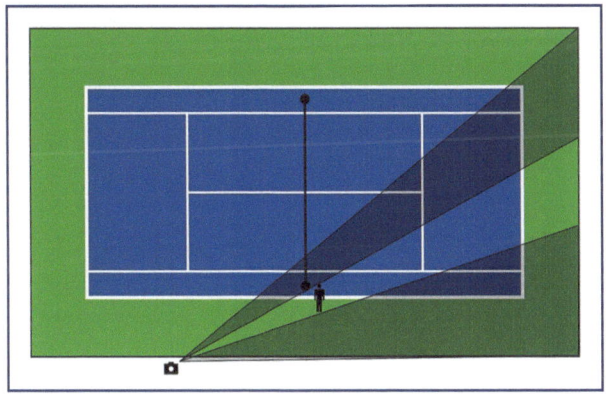

Figure 11
If a ball-person is blocking you, move so that he or she is blocking only your view to the center of the baseline. Hardly any interesting action happens there anyway.

in Chapter 1, you can't talk to the officials. So you can't ask a line judge or ballkid to move. (I've heard photographers do it anyway. I've even heard photographers yell at them and scold them for not complying. Please don't be one of those photographers.) You can't move the players' gear, and you certainly can't ask a chair umpire to move. And you also can't reasonably expect a television crew—which is paying handsomely to be there—to move, even if they could. So work around them all.

If ballkids are blocking one angle, aim for another. Or use the narrow visual range of a telephoto lens to shoot around or between them (see Figure 11) in the same way that you can isolate a player from unwanted elements in the background. Often I'll align myself so a ballkid is directly between me and the center of the baseline. Why? Because action very rarely happens there—I won't be shooting at that spot anyway.

If the ballkids and/or officials are obstructing you too much to effectively work around them, you have two options:

1. At the next changeover move to a spot where they won't be in your way (see Figure 12).

2. Wait a minute. Ballkids don't stay still for long. They'll chase balls and reposition themselves to other spots (hopefully in front of those cranky photographers). Even line umpires move; they'll

If you're positioned along the sideline, sometimes even two ball-people may block your view. But you can use a telephoto lens to shoot between them and isolate your subject (right, with a 630mm equivalent). Your angle of court coverage will be momentarily reduced, but be patient—ball-people always end up moving somewhere else.

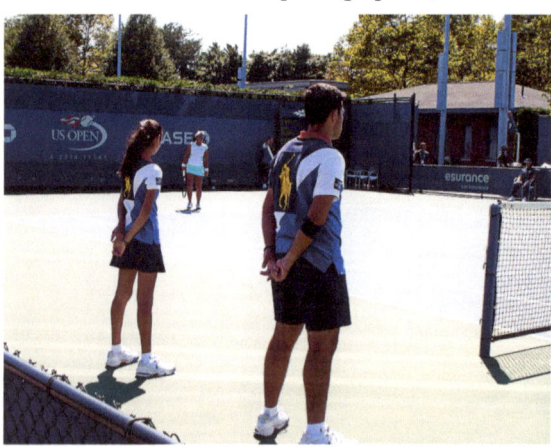
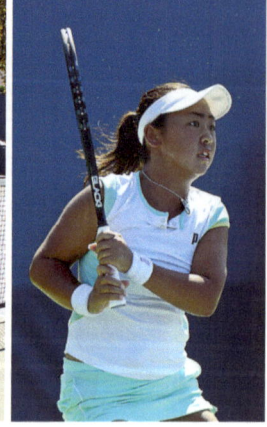

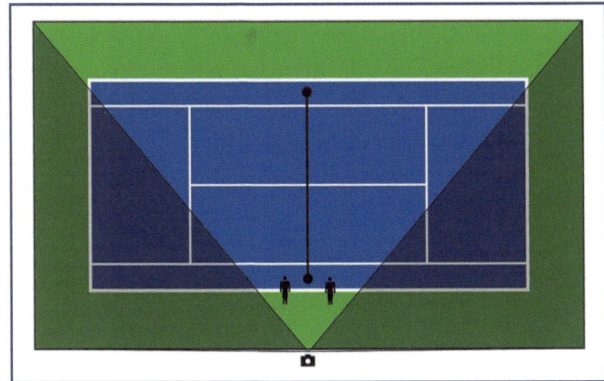

Figure 12
Sometimes the ballkids will seem to be in front of you constantly during a match, limiting your angles so much that you feel you're barely able to shoot. In those situations, I position myself right behind them; then at least I have a clear view of both ends of the baseline.

change ends and they'll change sides depending on which player is serving and to which side of the court.

Either way, don't fret the mobile officials. Sometimes they'll block you, but that's just part of the challenge of photographing tennis.

WHEN YOU'RE ASKED TO MOVE

No matter where you position yourself, even if it's in a legitimate spot, there's always a chance someone will object.

If a player asks you to move, grant the request. Whether he or she is a pro or an amateur, the fact remains that the court exists for tennis first.

If an official at a tournament asks you to move, grant the request. His or her job is to enforce the rules of the event, which are designed to give the players room to play, spectators room to see, and (lastly) photographers room to shoot.

If you're an un-credentialed photographer at a professional tournament and a credentialed photographer asks you to move, grant the request—*especially* if you're in a spot reserved for media. Most pros will be happy to share space in places where it's allowed (such as at side courts), and some might even offer tips if you ask. But they're there to work, and that should be respected.

Again, if you show others respect and you act professionally, you will likely be treated the same.

CHAPTER FOUR

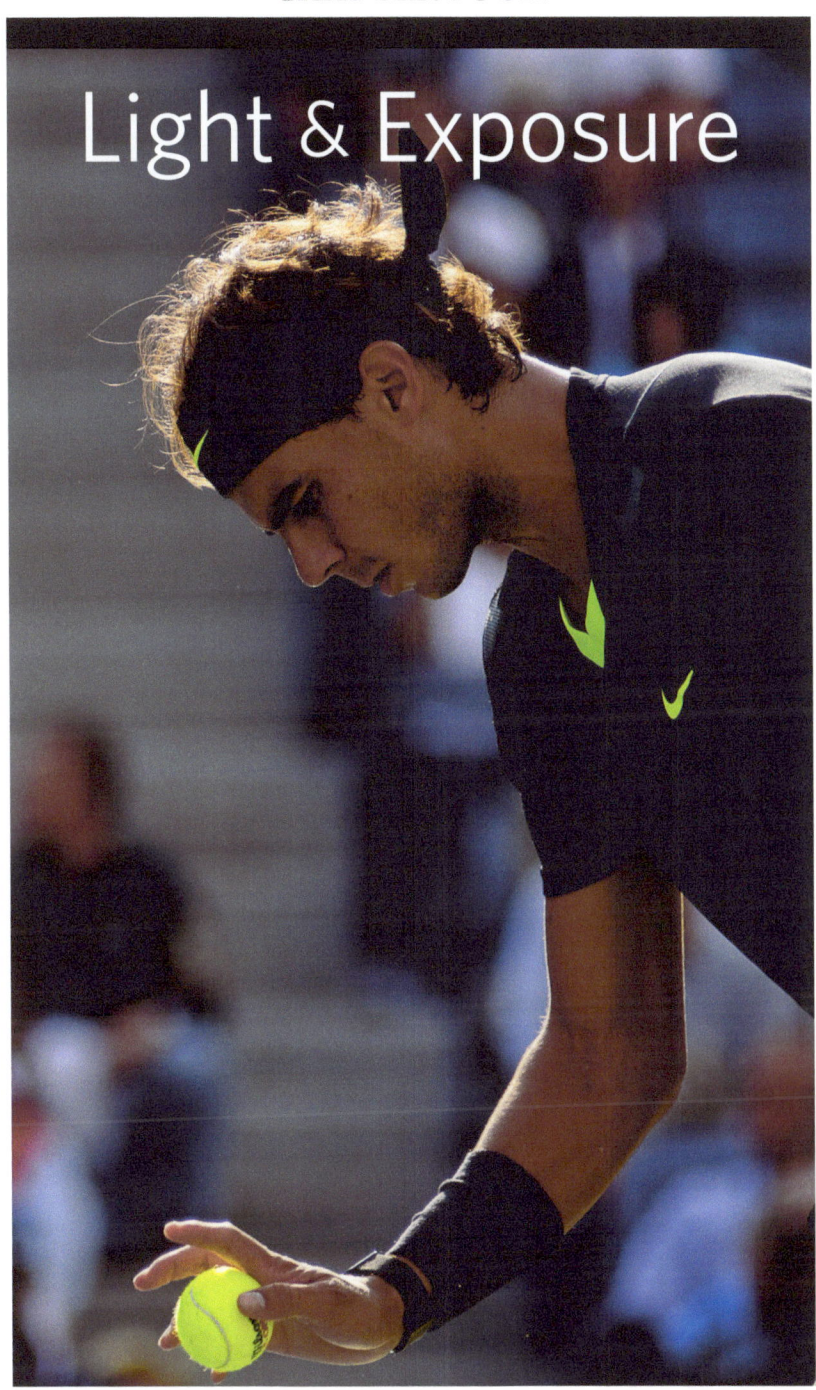

Light & Exposure

LIGHT & EXPOSURE

Shoot tennis outside. That's the priority when it comes to tennis photography and light. No indoor court in the world is illuminated with light of enough strength and quality to photograph tennis nearly as well as you can outside.

Yes, digital camera technology has drastically narrowed the gap between what's achievable with sunlight and artificial illumination. But cameras aren't magic. The sun is stronger than ceiling-mounted light bulbs, and it produces more contrast and more even tones across a scene. You can correct for a lack in these qualities in post-production, to an extent. However, the best camera in the world can't give you a shutter speed of 1/1000 at an ISO of 100 in a dome, nor in an arena. Moreover, indoor illumination will never allow you the opportunity to play with juxtapositions of light and shadow the way late-afternoon sunlight will.

TYPES OF LIGHT

Light comes in all sorts of tones and directions, all of which are at least somewhat useful for photographing tennis. I don't believe in avoiding certain light. Rather, the trick is knowing how to use each type of light effectively.

Front & Top Light

After indoor light, front light is probably the worst light for photographing tennis (and anything else). It allows for the fastest shutter speeds, but it also creates an image devoid of shadow. Shadow, as anyone who's studied photography probably knows, creates a sense of depth and definition to an image. Without shadow, the scene and the action will look flat.

Just as bad is top light. In tennis, light from close to directly above (such as at midday in the middle of the year) can cause some issues that are difficult to overcome. Many players will wear hats in these conditions, the brims of which will cast heavy shadows over their eyes. (Yes, in the last paragraph shadows were good; in this paragraph they're bad.

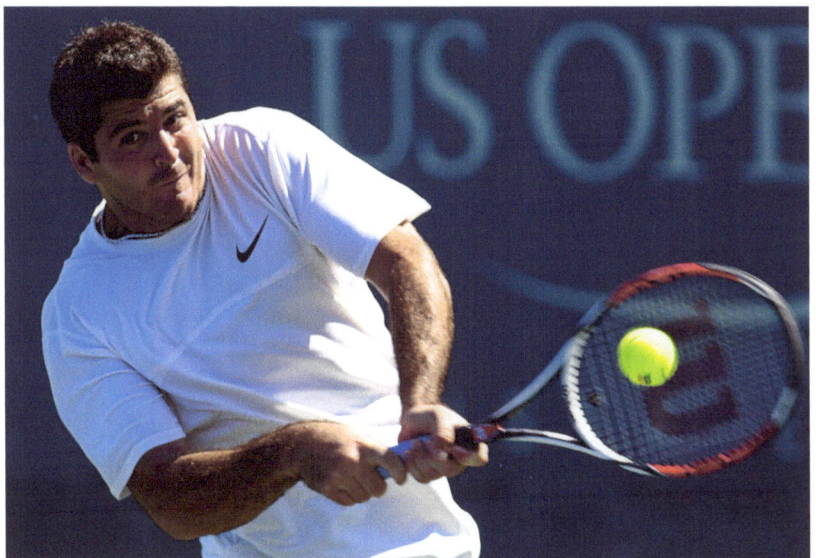

The difference is in whether they help or hurt a photo. If shadows are hiding a player's eyes, that's definitely not good.)

The darker the player's complexion, the worse this problem becomes. I know several photographers (including me, often) who won't even bother shooting Venus Williams in an early-afternoon match; her very dark skin combined with the white visor she wears on bright days makes an acceptable exposure impossible. In a portrait-shoot situation, you could compensate for this by using a flash, but in tennis that's not a permitted solution.

Should you never shoot in front light or top light? I'd hardly ever say never. As the old photographers' axiom dictates, if a Pulitzer Prize-winning photo is happening in front of you, just shoot. Aside from that, keep the sun off your back. Moving just a little—either to a different spot or just by rotating—can help you convert that front light into something that will help you much more: side light. If you're shooting from the sideline and you find that one player is front-lit, then look at the other side of the court—that player will be side-lit.

Likewise, you can use harsh midday light creatively by making the shadow part of your subject. You may find that shooting down on the action from an elevated position creates some nice effects (see the photo on page 55).

Side light is great for opening up shadows and adding depth to your subject.

Side Light

In terms of illumination and tennis photography, side light is a sweet spot. It's strong enough to allow you fast shutter speeds, but still gives you some shadow to work with. And note that light doesn't need to be coming from exactly a 90-degree angle to qualify—any angle that gives you some shadow-created definition will probably make you happy with how your photos turn out.

You'll still often need to deal with shadows on players' faces. If the sun is shining, many of them will be wearing hats or visors. This presents an exposure problem regardless of complexion. You can compensate for this somewhat by opening up the exposure at little (a third- or half-stop), but you need to be careful not to blow out other areas of the photo (a likely risk in strong light). You can also compensate by just watching the player's face; when hitting, his or her head will move somewhat, and you'll sometimes find an instant when the hat brim rises enough to allow light in.

Back Light

Shooting back-lit can help even out the tones between light and dark, letting a player's face come out from a hat's shadow.

If any light shares side light's "sweet spot" status in tennis photography, it's back light. I know some photographers who shoot all their tennis photos back-lit. I find that approach too monotonous, but I understand the temptation. Back light not only holds some particular advantages, but also solves some common problems.

Its main creative advantage is that it allows you to play with light in a different way. Back-lit photos tend to have a softer look and a unique aesthetic quality. Another creative benefit is that when you're shooting back-lit in stadiums, the crowd behind the action will sometimes be in shadow. This helps minimize the distractions in that otherwise busy background.

As much as back light gives you some more creative

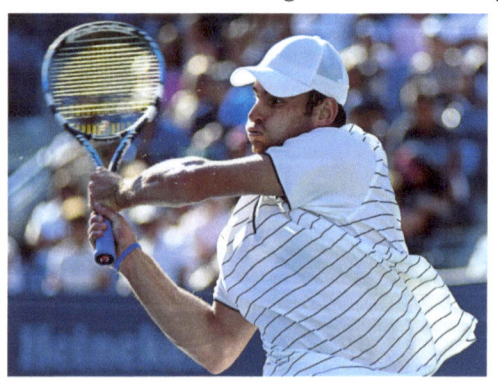

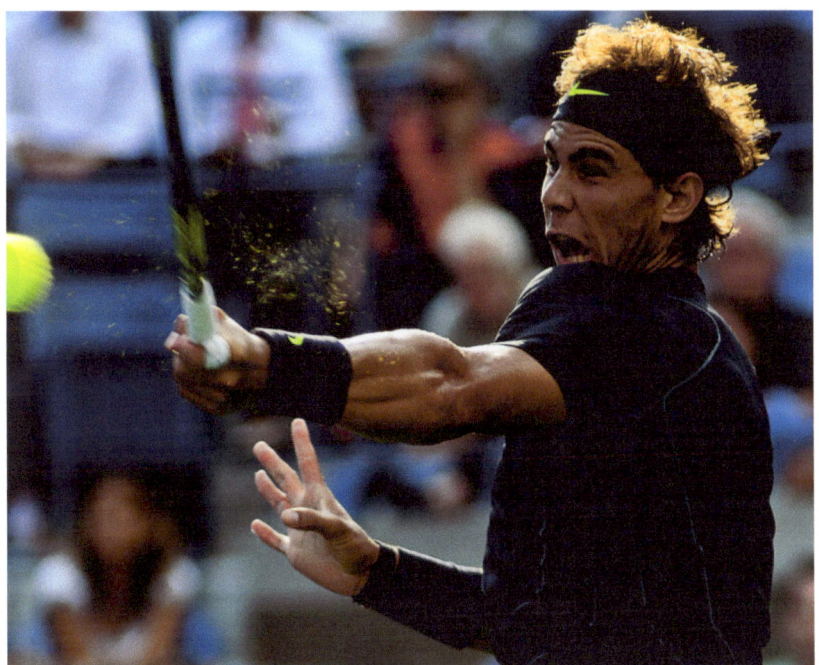

options, it also can help you shoot a dark-skinned player on a sunny day, or any player whose hat or visor is casting shadows on the face. To shoot back-lit, you have to open up your exposure a lot (by as much as two stops), otherwise the player will be almost completely darkened. By opening up that much, you'll "even out" the shadows — in other words, by opening up the shadow the player is standing in (his or her own), you also open up the shadow created by the brim of the hat. Back light can do such a great job of leveling tones that it will save your midday; those harsh, ugly shadows you try to avoid will all become just shade when the sun is behind the player. Open up your exposure, and you can have great-looking back-lit images.

With all these advantages, you may wonder why you shouldn't just always shoot tennis back-lit. Well, you can. As I've mentioned, I know photographers who do exactly that. However, that strategy presents two disadvantages. First, you would be forgoing the chance to have more variety in your images. Back-lit photos tend to have muted colors and a unique aesthetic. I wouldn't want *all* my images to look like that, particularly because a major component of my style is

You can use back light to produce a rim-light effect, where the sunrays catch the edges of a player's hair or the fuzz of the ball.

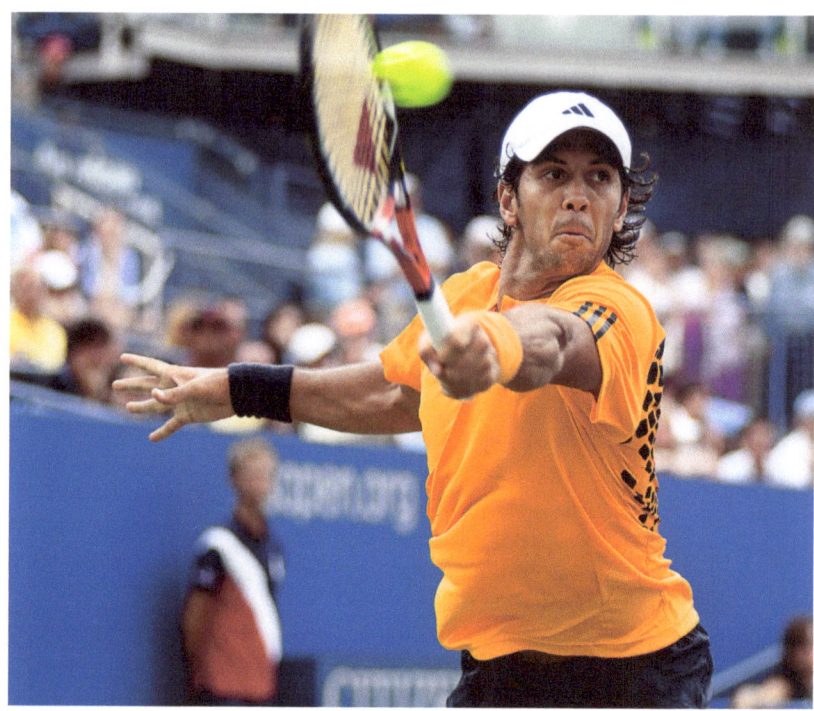

Overcast lighting is great for making tones more even. It's especially useful for shooting a player wearing a white hat that in brighter conditions could blow out and would cast a shadow on the face.

working with vivid color. Second, because of the required exposure adjustment, shooting back-lit means you have to sacrifice either shutter speed or ISO. In the coming pages, we'll see how losing either of those can be detrimental to your final product.

Gray Light

Gray light in overcast conditions is next on the list of preferred illumination for tennis. This light isn't bad; it does offer some advantages—primarily that it does an excellent job of equalizing the exposure between dark and light complexions, bright clothes and hat-brim shadows. It's also soft, which can create a pleasing effect for portrait-type photos of players. Its side effects are much the same as those of back light: somewhat muted colors, and reduced shutter speeds or higher ISOs.

Of course, unlike your choice between shooting in front light, side light or back light, overcast conditions don't give you an option—when the sky is overcast, it's overcast no matter which direction you face. Therefore, a big advantage is that your angle is not limited by the light; you can shoot from any position with almost the exact same exposure and the exact same look to the images.

Artificial Light

At the beginning of this chapter I relegated tennis photography to the outdoors. However, obviously there are times when you must shoot in artificial light, either inside or at night.

In those times, you will need to increase your ISO to at least 800. (Fortunately digital cameras do better at these high settings than they did even a couple of years ago, and exceedingly better than film ever did.) You will also find that achieving a shutter speed fast enough to freeze action will require very large apertures—probably f/2.8. So if you have to shoot in artificial light often, make sure you have adequate gear.

Also, shooting under lights often presents the challenge of color shifts. Shooting in daylight, your camera will usually record color accurately, even when your white balance is in "Auto" mode. The same won't apply to artificially lit photos—automatic white balance will usually result in some odd shifts in your color. However, you do have ways to combat this.

First, there are numerous ways to determine which white-balance setting is best for the light while you're shooting. You can get a good idea by trying different settings and looking at the results on your camera's LCD. Alternatively, you can use a color meter (which I've never seen someone do in tennis—that tactic is mainly for studio work, and is also largely a relic of the film era) or an in-field calibration tool (such as the Xrite ColorChecker or the ColorRight white-balance filter).

You can also adjust the color in post-production. This is the option I recommend, because it's easy, accurate and doesn't require toting any extra gear in your bag. By using software such

Artificial light was once terrible to shoot in, but no longer. The light hasn't changed, rather the gear has. Today's cameras are much better at capturing nice images in weaker light.

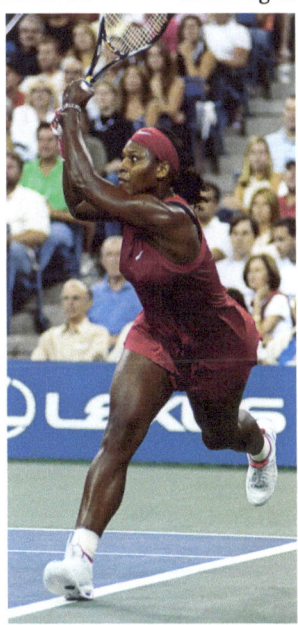

Juxtaposing Light

Dark shadows don't always have to be avoided. On the contrary, they can also be used creatively. If you can manage your angle so that you're photographing the action in bright light while the background is completely in shadow, then

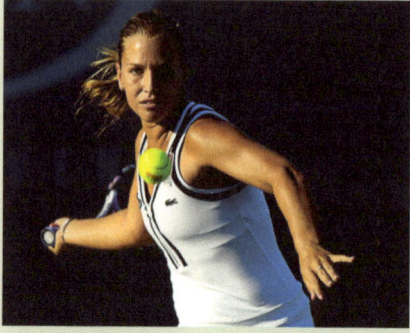

your subject will "pop" dramatically. Fortunately the tennis environment, with all its windscreens and stands and such, presents this opportunity more frequently than you might find in other sports.

In fact, my favorite time to shoot at a big tournament with lots of side courts is late afternoon or early evening. Shadows can be found everywhere, especially along the backscreens, while the players are lit with the warm "magic hour" light that photographers have written entire books about. Juxtaposing the two creates what might be the best lighting condition in photography.

Apply that to photographing tennis, and you can make some stunning action images. So when you're looking for nice light, look for shadows, too.

as Lightroom or Aperture, you can color-correct an entire shoot with one click.

EXPOSURE

Hold onto your monopod—I'm about to write two things that might not seem to belong together:

1. Tennis and the environments it's played in present inordinate challenges to determining the ideal exposure for photographs. The sun is usually bright, which causes shadows to be solid black; usually this would indicate that you want to overexpose a little. The players often wear white on at least part of their outfits; usually this would warrant under-exposing a little. They also wear hats, which cast shadows on the face; usually this

would call for over-exposing a little. At a pro tournament, they will sometimes be playing in front of a crowd that's in shadow; usually this would call for under-exposing a little. You can see the problem.

2. When photographing tennis, you should use manual exposure.

The second point is where you might get upset with me. "Wait a second," you may say. "With all these contradicting exposure variables in the scene, you want me to figure out the exposure *myself*? Instead of letting the camera's *computer* do it?"

Yes. You should shoot in manual mode *because* of all the contradicting variables. No matter how advanced your camera's exposure meter is, it can't know what you want to do with the myriad shadows and highlights in a typical tennis scene. Determining your own exposure will allow you to control those issues, and thereby control the quality of your tennis photos. This requires a little more thinking, but it's worth the effort.

In a brightly-lit tennis scene, a camera sensor usually cannot record detail in both shadows and highlights. Therefore, you often need to pick one to sacrifice. Either you let the shadows go completely black, or you let the highlights go completely white (i.e., blow out). Do the first one—let the shadows go. In tennis photography, important visual information is almost never found in the shadows, so you don't lose much by letting them go. On the other hand, the highlights are usually part of your subject—perspiration-coated skin, white stripes on a shirt, white tennis shoes, and so on. You want to keep those areas from blowing out. Otherwise, when printed, those spots will look empty, or fake, or "just wrong."

Tennis scenes are often filled with extremes that can throw off your camera's meter: bright sunlight, shadows, white clothes and hats, bright spots in dark backgrounds, and so on.

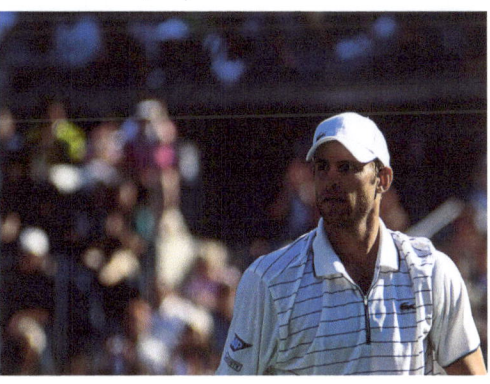

Ignoring Blow Outs

When determining exposure, you almost always want to avoid highlights from blowing out. However, you'll come across two exceptions to that rule.

First, when shooting back-lit, you will have to *allow* for blown-out highlights — in hair, in the racquet strings, at the edge of clothing, even in the fuzz around the edges of the ball. You could try to compensate in post-production, but that would reduce the contrast so much that the image would look, quite literally, surreal. So don't worry about it. These blow-outs are okay because the viewer's eyes will expect them.

Also, you'll encounter situations wherein trying to eliminate highlights seems impossible or impractical. At those times, at least control where the blow-outs occur. If they're in parts of the photo that aren't important, or where they're not too much of a distraction, then it may be okay (if not ideal) to leave them.

(The exception to this is when you're shooting with back light, as discussed on page 70. In that case, you need to decide how much to let the highlights blow out so that you can achieve a realistic-looking exposure of the player's face and body. I usually under-expose a little so I can save *some* of the detail in the highlights, then brighten the mid-tones in post-production; this involves extra work, but it's generally worth the effort for images that are publication-bound.)

This goal is best achieved in manual-exposure mode. In automatic modes, the camera will look for an average exposure, which will almost definitely let the highlights blow out in every image. To combat this, you *could* use automatic exposure in conjunction with a camera's exposure-compensation feature to correct the camera's propensity to over-expose the highlights. However, I don't like the idea of using exposure compensation as a general setting. In the midst of shooting, especially in the busy atmosphere of a tennis court, you can easily forget you've made the adjustment, thereby affecting all your exposures once you've moved on from a particular angle or location. Besides, if you're going to that much trouble, you might as well just set the exposure yourself.

However, I do suggest you use your camera's assistance. Most modern DSLRs have two tools that will make finding your ideal exposure relatively easy: the histogram and highlight warnings.

THE HISTOGRAM

A histogram is a bar chart of the tones in your scene. The left end is a measurement of the blacks (shadows), the right is a measurement of the whites (highlights), and in between is a measurement of all the mid-tones.

The histogram is the light meter of the 21st century—it reveals everything you need to know about your exposure. If your exposure has no clogged shadows, then the curve of that bar chart will tail off nicely and end before it reaches the left of the histogram; likewise, if there are no blown-out highlights, then the curve will end before it reaches the right. However, if the curve ends abruptly at the left—in sort of a sharp, steep wall—then that means there was more dark information in your scene than was recorded, and your

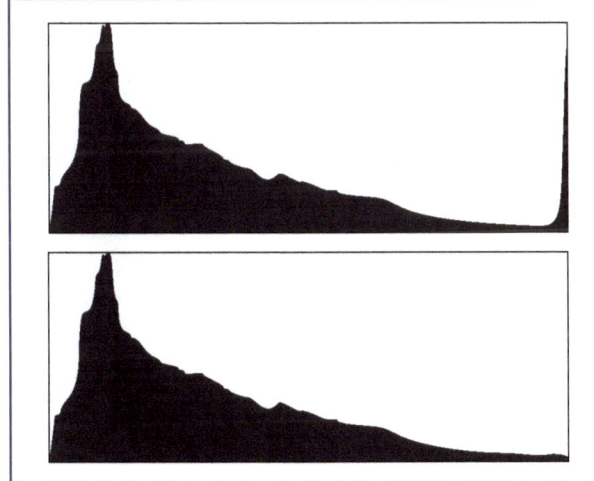

Figure 13
If you see your histogram data "piling up" at the right, your image has blown-out highlights (top). The histogram of a good exposure will generally tail off nicely on both ends (bottom).

shadows have gone black; likewise, if the curve walls up against the right, then your highlights are blown out. The latter is what we're most concerned about; we don't want to lose details in the highlights (see Figure 13).

Therefore, in order avoid blown-out highlights, you want to ensure that the exposure you choose does not cause the histogram to pile up on the right side of the curve.

HIGHLIGHT WARNINGS

Many cameras have an option to show highlight warnings (also affectionately known as "the blinkies") on the LCD. With this option on, when you review your images in-camera, any area that is blown-out will flash (see Figure 14). If areas are flashing that you don't want blown out, then you know to either close down your aperture, increase your shutter speed or decrease your ISO — in other words, cut the amount of light the sensor is recording.

These tools in a digital camera are so effective at helping you determine an exposure that an actual hand-held light meter has practically become a relic in most genres of photography. I haven't carried a meter in my bag in years, and I can't remember the last time I saw a tennis photographer use one.

However, when you use these tools to help avoid blown-out highlights, you do risk a side-effect: Dark photos. You can compensate for this by adjusting the brightness in your

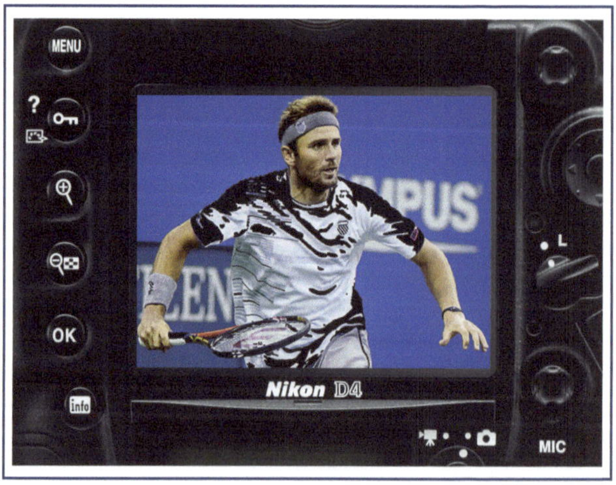

Figure 14

When enabled on your camera's LCD, the black (or sometimes red) "blinkies" will indicate areas of your image that are blown out. Some blinkies can be okay, such as those in specular highlights, or at the edges of a player who's backlit. How much photo real estate is acceptable to have blown out? That's a creative decision for you to make.

post-production software. (Adjust brightness, not exposure; the latter will re-blow out your highlights, while the former will bring up only the mid-tones.)

Is this more work than simply putting your camera in auto-exposure mode and hoping its mistakes aren't too detrimental? Yes. But taking control and doing the extra work (which isn't all that much if you're using Lightroom or Aperture) will make your photos better.

You do not, of course, need to go through all of this for every photo. When shooting tennis, you'll likely have your camera pointed in one direction for long blocks of time. Once you do change your position, or your angle, only then will you need to re-check and adjust your exposure. In time, the process will become intuitive and quick.

IGNORING THIS ADVICE

After this explanation, if you still want to use auto-exposure, then go right ahead. Today's cameras will do a better job than last decade's would have. Still, you *will* see mixed results. If you can, stick with shooting at an angle that minimizes extreme light and dark tones, so that your frame is filled with mostly mid-tones. Then your auto-exposed photos will look good more consistently.

Also, avoid Aperture Priority and Program (fully automatic) modes. Those will change your shutter speed, which you want to maintain absolute control over. In many areas of photography, your primary camera-based creative control is the aperture. But in tennis it's the shutter.

Ideal Shutter Speeds

Each sport has "ideal" shutter speeds for photography. Usually it's okay to shoot at speeds faster than the ideal (except perhaps for auto racing, for which blur is usually beneficial). But shoot slower than ideal, and you start to have problems (or artistic genius, depending on your point of view).

In tennis, as with most sports, you have a creative option regarding whether to freeze or slightly blur the action. If your goal is art, then you may want to blur; if your goal is anything else, then you probably want to freeze, or at least

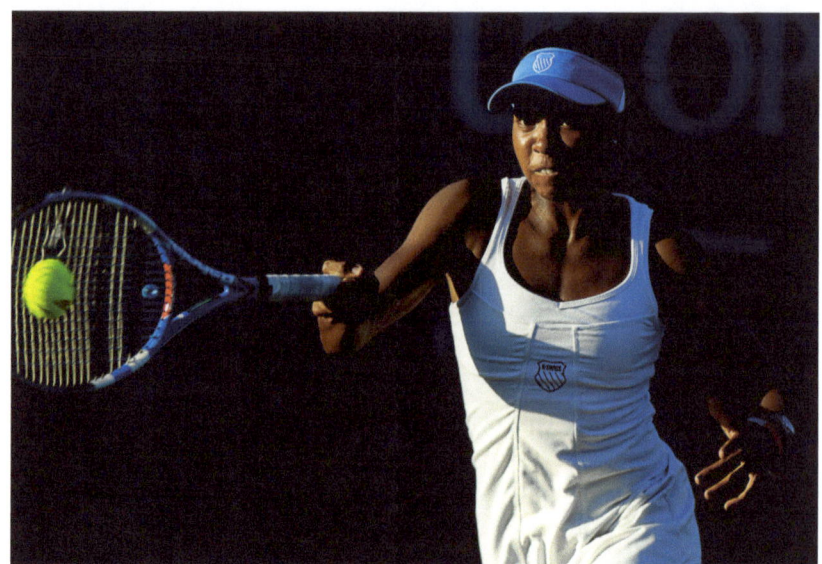

If you want to capture the ball hitting the racquet, you'll need a lot of luck and a fast shutter speed (for this photo, 1/2000).

come close to freezing. And in tennis, freezing the action takes an extremely fast shutter speed.

The pro players, of course, require the fastest shutter speeds of all, because they run the fastest and hit the hardest. When shooting a men's or women's tour event, in order to freeze the action, try not to shoot at speeds slower than 1/800. You can be successful at 1/640, but almost always with blur. If you must shoot at a slower shutter speed, then the trick is to use the blur in a way that helps the image rather than hinders it, or to shoot from an angle where the blur is less apparent. For example, if you're shooting from a 90-degree angle to the player, a hard forehand stroke will be moving incredibly fast through your frame—so fast that it will barely render at 1/640. At 1/400 the effect might be that the racquet isn't even visible, that you've merely photographed a person waving a blurry arm through the air. However, at a slighter angle (say, 25 degrees), the same forehand will move through less of the frame, creating less blur. That effect can actually be quite pleasing, lending a slight sense of motion to the image.

If you do decide to *slightly* blur the photos, you'll probably need to be shooting in the range of 1/640 to 1/1000. You'll also want to be careful to blur only the action (the ball, the racquet, a little of the arm), not the player's face.

If you want to completely freeze pro-tennis action, then you probably need to be shooting at 1/1600 or faster. If you have enough light and a large enough aperture, you can increase that more. Shooting with very fast shutter speeds can produce stunningly sharp images with no apparent blur in either the ball or the racquet. This is an effect you may or may not like; some photographers love to freeze the action to capture a perfect, tiny slice of time, while others like including a slight blur to create the aforementioned sense of motion. The choice can be a simple preference, or can be dictated by the intended use of the photo. For example, if you're trying to illustrate what happens to a tennis ball upon impact with the racquet (it collapses to about a third of its diameter), you'll want to freeze as much as possible.

However, this all assumes optimal conditions. If you're working on a cloudy day, you might not have enough light to shoot at 1/1600. That leaves you with two options: Boost your ISO (which you may not want to do, depending on how well your camera performs in low light), or get creative with blur. This is a good reason to learn to work with blur even if that's not your preferred style.

When you're photographing amateur players, figure that you can shoot an extra third-stop slower for every level down from pro. College players and elite juniors hit a little softer than pros; low-level juniors and

Different shutter speeds can completely freeze the action (left, shot at 1/2500) or allow some blur to give a sense of motion (right, 1/800).

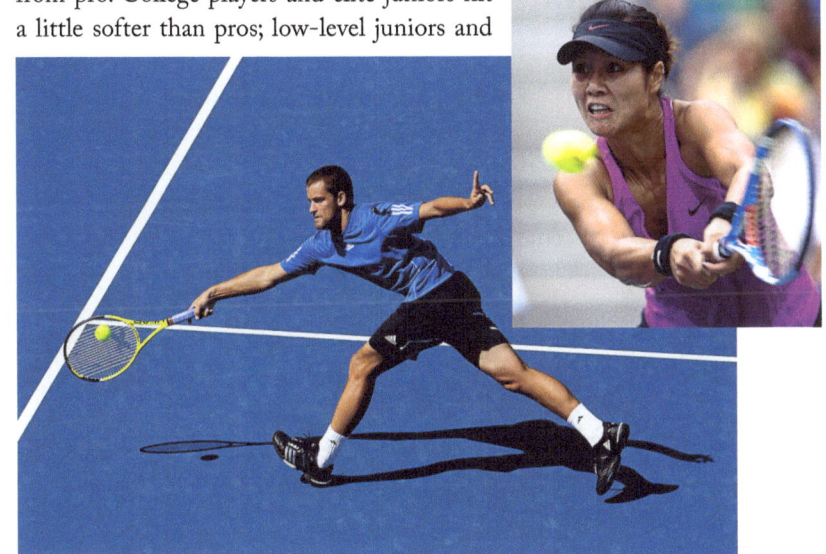

recreational adults hit a little softer still. When photographing children playing tennis, I've shot at shutter speeds as slow as 1/250 and frozen the action effectively.

The point is that these shutter speeds are neither absolute nor definitive. Every player is different, every type of stroke is different, and shooting from different angles affects the result. Therefore, the following chart is meant only as a guide, advice for a starting point to determine how fast you want your shutter to be in different situations.

	Pro	Amateur/Jr.	Child
Freeze	1/1600+	1/1000+	1/500+
Some Blur	1/800	1/500	1/180
Blur	1/500-	1/320-	1/60-

Determining the exact shutter speed at which you will freeze or blur action to your liking is not a science. (Well, it could be. But that would require a speed gun, a sextant and a calculator, none of which, you may recall, did I recommend carrying in your bag in Chapter 2.) However, today's photographer does have one very advanced tool that can help find ideal shutter speeds: the digital camera. The LCD, alas, reveals your results. Too much blur? Increase your shutter speed. Too frozen? Decrease your shutter speed. After your first test exposure in a specific situation, no guesswork is needed.

Ideal Apertures

Your ideal aperture will be easier to determine. Because you will probably often be trying to achieve the fastest shutter speeds possible for the light conditions, you'll probably want to be shooting with your lens nearly or completely wide open. I know some photographers who shoot at f/2.8 all the time; I like to shoot at f/4 (or even f/4.5) if I can, just to create an extra sliver of depth of field. I hardly ever have an exposure in tennis that involves a smaller aperture than that.

However, another reason to work with large apertures is to control the background (see "Backgrounds" on page 56). Just about every tennis court is surrounded by things that are bad for the background of a photo. A wide aperture will allow you to blur these undesirables, which can reduce their cluttering effect.

For example, if you're shooting a pro tournament, your background may be bleachers full of fans. Shooting at f/2.8

Creativity

All these guidelines about aperture and shutter speed can also be used in reverse, for the sake of creativity. Feel free to experiment in every way. Close down the aperture. Slow down the shutter speed. Adjust the lens so it's out-of-focus. Shoot when the player's back is turned. Let the ball fall in a compositionally unconventional spot. In fact, break every rule I've outlined and see where the deviance leads you. Art is not about doing what everyone else does; it's about seeing what *you* can do.

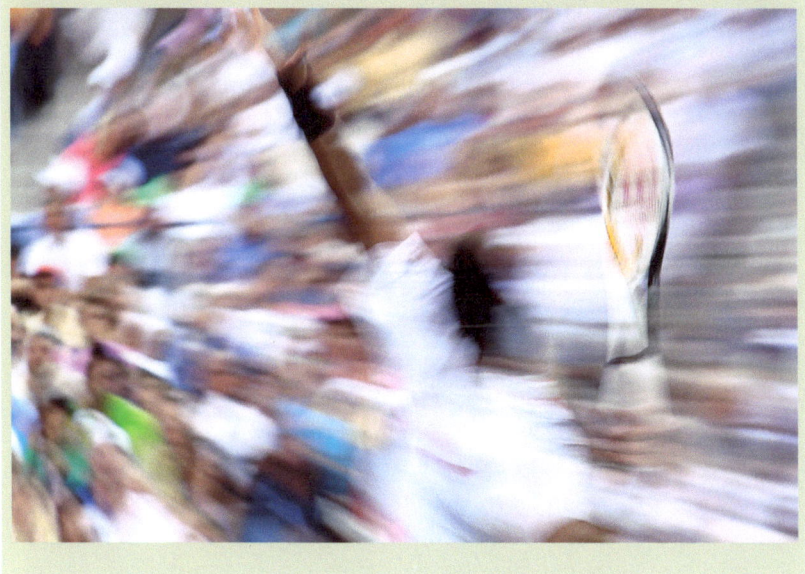

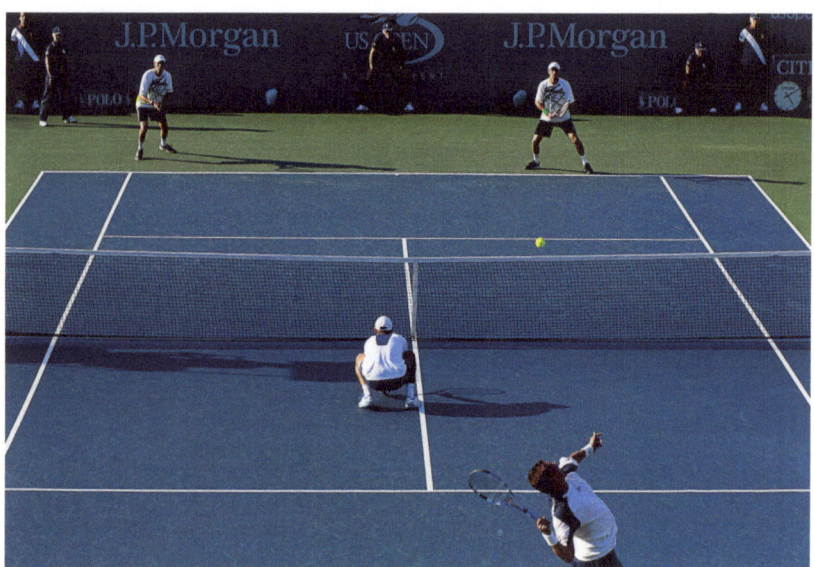

A rare f/8 photo from my tennis catalog. The greater depth of field helped keep the whole scene sharp, from the server to the officials along the backscreen.

can throw them so out of focus that they become just blobs of color—which can make for a very pleasing background (see the photo on page 112). If you're shooting at a public park, then trees, fences and such can present the same problem, and the same strategy can render the problem just as moot.

So you can see how aperture presents another push-and-pull dilemma when photographing tennis. Sometimes your want for blurring the action can produce an unsatisfactory background. Or your want for freezing the action can limit your ability to keep a background element in enough focus to have it be recognizable. In situations such as these, you have to choose which effect is more important to you—or shoot a little of both.

SHOOTING IN MIXED LIGHT

Earlier I wrote about shooting in different types of light. One thing I didn't mention was that all that advice assumed "perfect-world" lighting scenarios. It assumed that the sky would be either clear or cloudy, as if those states are binary.

In the real world, however, we have what meteorologists call "partly cloudy" or "mostly cloudy"—when even on a bright, blue-sky day, white clouds of myriad shapes and sizes float above us. As you know, on their journey, they often block the sun. This, of course, changes your exposure.

For a photographer shooting outdoor tennis and setting his or her exposure manually, this situation can be maddening. A thick cloud moving between you and the sun can cut the light hitting the court by more than two stops. Exactly how much depends on the location of the sun in the sky (sunlight coming from a lower angle will pass through more atmospheric particles, reducing its intensity), and the thickness and density of the cloud (is it blocking all direct light, or just diffusing it?). Your 1/1000-at-f/4 setting could suddenly, in the middle of a point, cause a considerable underexposure.

Moreover, by the time you adjust your shutter speed or aperture or ISO (or any combination thereof), checking for blown-out highlights in the process, the sun could pop back out again, rendering your new mental calculations useless.

To combat this, you could try shooting in Aperture Priority mode, which would automatically adjust to the changing conditions. However, you would almost certainly end up with blown-out highlights and bad exposures. You could also just stop shooting during the cloudy or sunny moments (depending on your shooting preference).

Or you could do this: Alternate between exposures. In other words, know your cloudy exposure and know your sunny exposure, and then switch between the two as needed.

How do you do this? When the thickest and densest of clouds is blocking the sun, determine a workable exposure, and remember it. Then when the cloud is gone and your scene is fully sunlit, determine another workable exposure and remember that, too. Consider everything you normally would—blown-out highlights, freezing or blurring the action, acceptable depth of field, and so on—even if your results vary in the different types of light.

Those two different readings become your end points, the opposite sides of the exposure spectrum you'll work

Blue skies with big, puffy clouds are pretty to look at but can be frustrating to shoot under. Every time a cloud obscures or reveals the sun, your exposure changes.

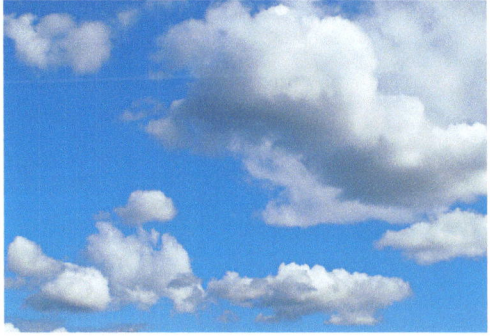

within. As the light changes from minute to minute, you can move between those two exposures, already knowing that each will accurately produce the effect you want.

To make this process easier, try to keep the change to just one of the three exposure variables, so that you need to alter only one setting as the light changes. For example, if both exposures have the same ISO and shutter speed, then you need to alter only the aperture when the light changes. Or, if you want complete control over motion *and* depth of field, then adjust only the ISO as the light changes.

To illustrate, let's assume that your ideal exposure in full sunlight is 1/2000 at f/4 with an ISO of 200. Then, with a cloud blocking the sun your ideal exposure is 1/800 at f/2.8 at the same ISO. You've memorized those two end-points, so you know which exposure to use in each lighting scenario, and you can alternate between the two while never having to pause shooting.

As you get more experienced doing this, you'll find it easier to decide where to stop between those two end-point exposures as the light changes in slighter grades. For example, if a thinner cloud temporarily blocks the sun, maybe your exposure becomes 1/1250 at f/2.8.

Also with experience, you'll find it easier to alternate exposures using a combination of ISO, aperture and shutter speed (rather than just one of them), which will avail more creative options. So if your full-light exposure is 1/2000 at f/4 with an ISO of 200, your cloud-cover exposure could be 1/1000 at f/3.5 at an ISO of 400, thereby allowing you to still freeze some action without giving up all your depth of field.

To the beginner, this may sound unnecessarily complicated. In fact, I realize that it can sound ridiculous to even attempt. But with practice, the ways that exposure variables affect one another become second-nature. Developing this kind of mental tool can make even an advanced photographer better.

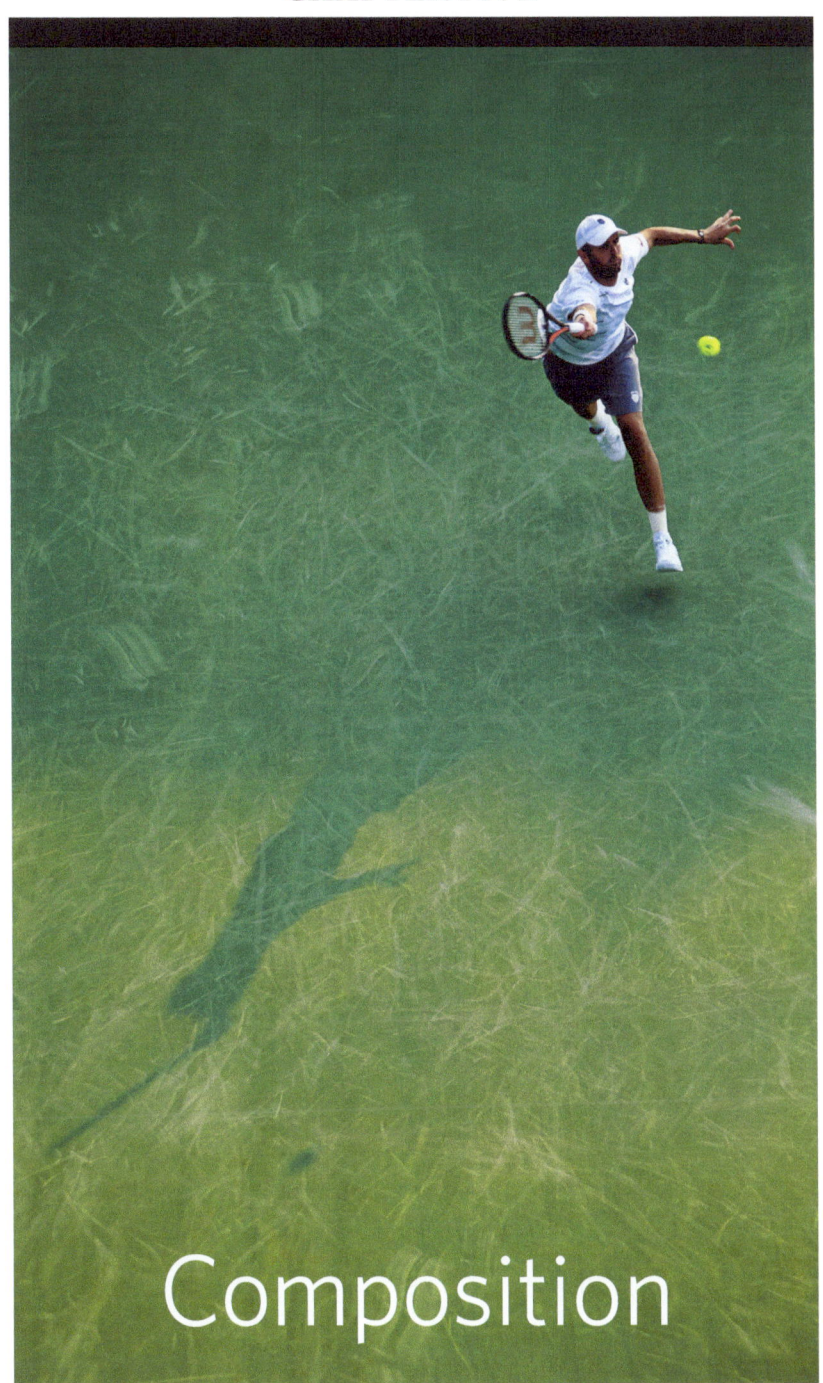

CHAPTER FIVE

Composition

COMPOSITION

Sometimes someone new to sports photography gets so caught up in capturing the action that he or she may forget that there's more to a photograph than just the subject. There's also composition, making the photo look good.

All the standard rules of composition also work for tennis photography: the rule of thirds, points of highest contrast, leading lines, and so on. They can just be a little harder to apply when all your subjects are running from place to place trying to hit a little yellow ball.

HORIZONTAL VS. VERTICAL

If you're in the middle of the woods in a National Park shooting a waterfall, you can switch between horizontal and vertical compositions pretty much at will. When you're shooting sports, however, changing your orientation mid-action isn't always so simple—and in tennis it's usually impossible.

Why? Because tennis is pretty stingy with time. It doesn't leave you much opportunity to change your setup when you notice that something different than what you're expecting is about to happen in front of you. In the short time required to simply move your hand, rotate the camera and reposition your finger over the shutter-release, you will likely have already missed the shot.

If you have a camera with two shutter-release buttons (such as a dedicated release on a vertical grip), you can increase your odds of success by using just one of them. You can turn the camera anytime you want and already have your finger in position to shoot. This way your grip on the camera never has to change, just the angle at which you hold your hand. However, this strategy often requires you to hold your wrist bent at a 90-degree angle for extended periods, which is a great way to develop tendonitis (I know this from experience). So you'd want to stay in that wrist-bent position only for short durations.

If you feel you must switch orientations in the midst of the action, either your intuition will need to be well developed or you'll need to be lucky. Honestly, you'll have to hope for both.

Therefore, the option that will deliver the most predictable results is to decide on a point-by-point basis whether to shoot either horizontal or vertical photos, and hope your choice is right. Often it won't be. Often you'll find that you could have made a great photo if your camera was oriented differently. This happens all the time in the photo pit at a pro event: In a gaggle of photographers, only a few will get a great shot because the others were either oriented wrong or had the wrong lens on the camera. You just have to learn to forget the photos you miss and enjoy the fact that by the end of the match you will have made more good photos by adhering to one approach than you would have made by trying to instantly adjust for every opportunity that flashed in front of you. The longer you stick with a setup, the better chance you'll get the shot you're hoping for.

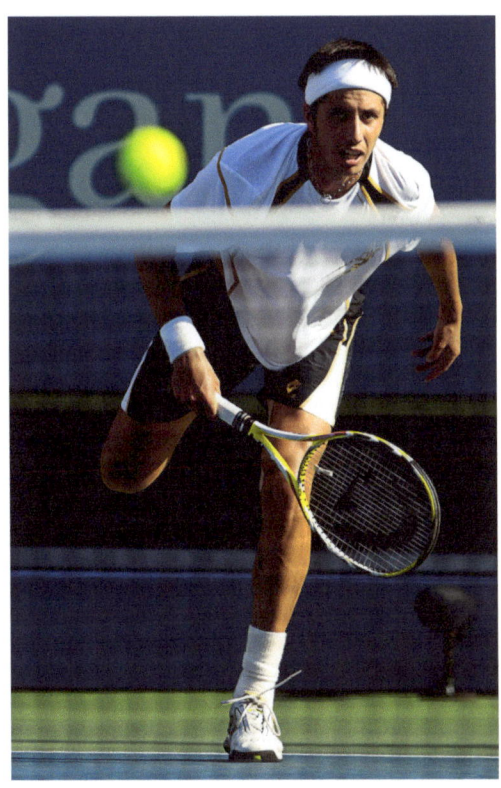

Vertical format is natural for tennis photography, because the human form is vertical. Subsequently, it's ideal for full-body photos.

How do you decide between the two orientations? On the big moments of a match—match points, set points, and even important break or hold points—you'll have to use experience and knowledge of the game and of the players to make your best guess.

For example, if you were shooting Pete Sampras hitting a first serve to end a set, you might know that he had no fear of coming to net to try to win a decisive point quickly. So, if you were sitting near mid-court with a 300mm lens, you might deduce that horizontal framing would allow the best opportunity for getting Sampras' face, ball and racquet all in the same shot on a potential volley (see the photo on page 133). In the same situation, but with a 70-200mm lens on the camera, you might try vertical framing, knowing that Sampras may have to leap for an overhead. In both instances, you are still not likely to get the shot you are hoping for, because dozens of other scenarios could play out instead; what's important is that you know the most likely of those scenarios and put yourself in the best circumstance to make a successful photo—before Sampras even serves the ball. Alternatively, you might even attach a wide-angle lens to the camera and frame horizontally, hoping Sampras dives toward your position for a wide passing shot. In that case, you will have set up a low-yield situation, prepared for a scenario that is unlikely, but, if it did occur, could give you a portfolio-worthy result.

However, a majority of every tennis match is played far away from big moments. The second serve of the third point of the fourth game of the first set is hardly ever a time for much excitement. So during most of the action you can decide between horizontal and vertical framing based simply on what type of photo you want to make at the moment. If you're looking for full-body ground strokes, you'll probably

... vs. Diagonal

You can also think outside of the level box. No law says you have to photograph tennis with an even horizon. In fact, shooting with diagonal framing can produce

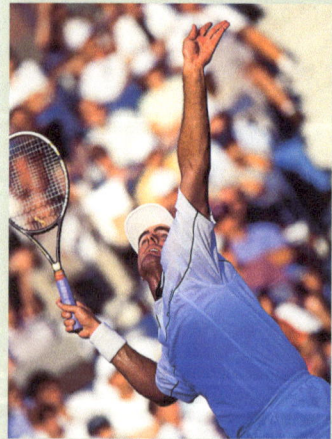

some interesting and unexpected results. But if you try this, be sure you're not doing it just to be different. Use the angle to help improve the composition, or to help produce a composition that might not be possible with a more traditional approach.

For example, in this photo (left) I turned the camera about 30 degrees so that I could frame the server's arm parallel with the edge of the photo. The effect is that the viewer encounters an unexpected angle of view, but that angle is still anchored to an element of the scene.

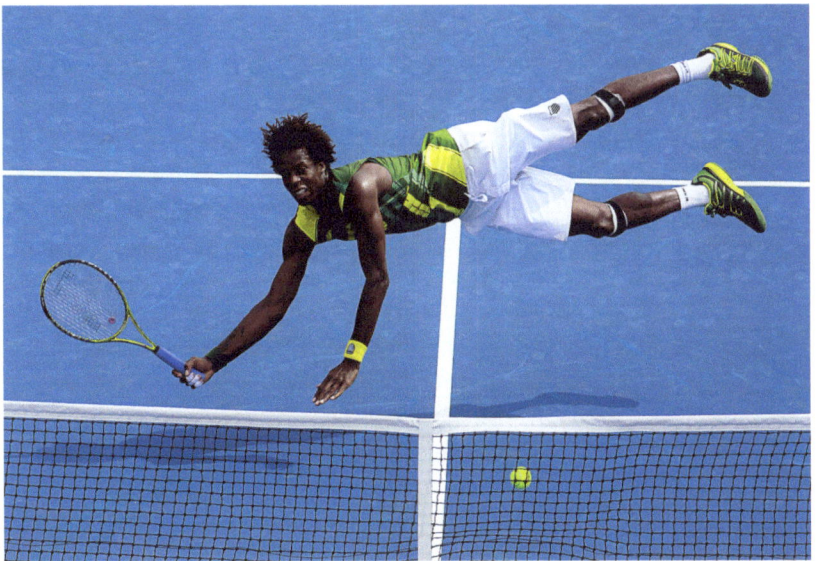

frame vertically; if you're looking for tightly-framed back-hands, you might want to frame horizontally.

Horizontal
orientation
can work great
for action that
"stretches out"
across the frame.

The choice between horizontal and vertical is really based on the same criteria for photographing anything, including waterfalls in the forests of national parks: Where is most of the subject, and how will it best fall within the frame in a compositionally pleasing way? What is in the background, and does part of it need to be excluded from the image? Where will the ball be when the player is about to make contact? And so on.

How a particular shot should (or could) be best framed is not always obvious. So even if you've chosen to shoot one way, use your camera's LCD to critique your results; look to see if you could be making different or better photos from the same angle by just rotating your camera a quarter turn. Or just turn the camera, shoot, and see what you get.

FRAMING

At the beginning of my tennis-photography career, I kept thinking I was doing something wrong. I'd sit at a match and study how to shoot a certain stroke. I'd learn lessons every time—lessons about where to aim the camera, how to frame a certain shot, how to adjust framing to anticipate the player's movement, how to compose to keep his or her hands and arms and head and the tennis ball in the same photo. But when I returned to the court later, those lessons often didn't seem to work anymore. So I'd readjust and relearn the lessons, just to later find them failing yet again.

The variable I wasn't applying was simple: the player. The lesson I really needed to learn was that different players look different when they're playing, in just about every regard. They move their bodies differently, prepare for hitting certain strokes differently, follow through with their racquets differently, recover from shots differently, and even make contact with the ball in different locations. So while the first lesson in framing tennis action is to comprehend the basics of how certain strokes look in photographs, the second lesson is seeing how those basics differ from player to player. This is true at every level of the game, from juniors to adults to seniors, from the recreational to the developmental to the professional. Therefore, I obviously can't write an unabridged guide to photographing every possible play in tennis. The variations are infinite.

The only perfect guide to learning this is experience: shooting hundreds or thousands of frames of every stroke and every play you can possibly see on a tennis court. Experience will dictate how to react to the instantaneous changes and plays in the game; experience will determine when to go wide or tight, horizontal or vertical, in the middle of a point. After more than 15 years, I still botch this all the time. No photographer can ever be perfect at it. But you can do much to better your odds. You can *practice*.

What I can do is offer some guidance on how to approach composition in a general way, and propose some tips on how to adapt to the play of certain types of players.

Cropping Body Parts

The world has two types of people: Those who divide people into two groups, and those who don't. You can also divide the population another way: Those who are willing to crop off body parts in a photo, and those who aren't. The question seems to never go away: Does a successful action

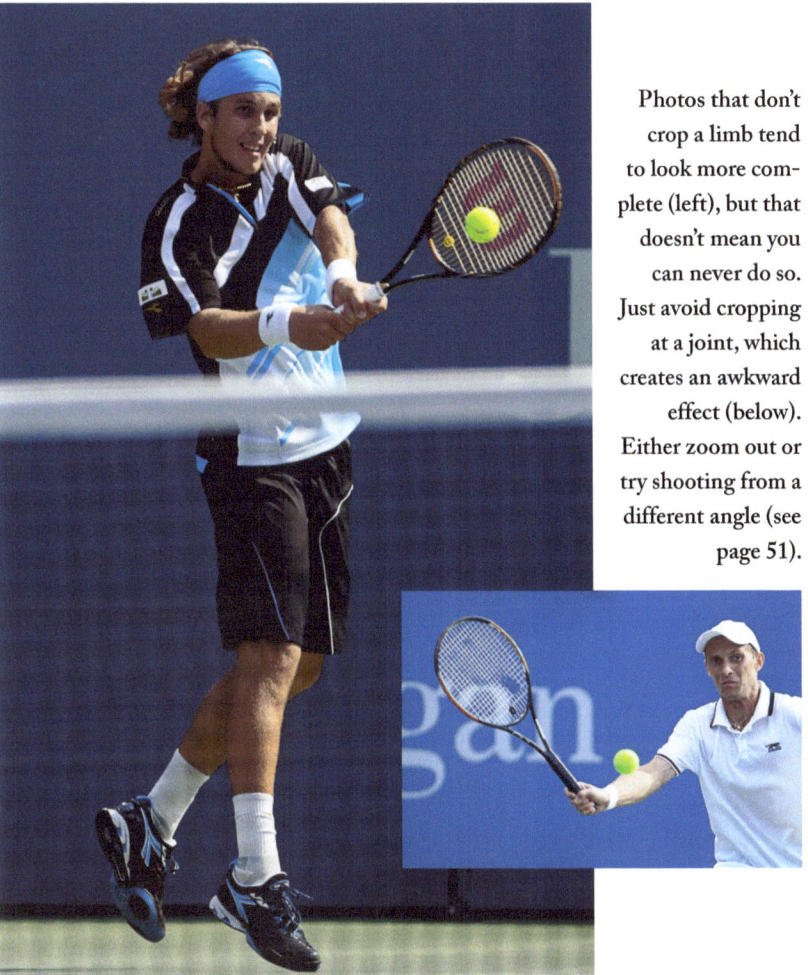

Photos that don't crop a limb tend to look more complete (left), but that doesn't mean you can never do so. Just avoid cropping at a joint, which creates an awkward effect (below). Either zoom out or try shooting from a different angle (see page 51).

photo need to include every body part, or is it okay for an arm or a leg to be cut off at the edge of the frame? The answer, of course, is both.

The matter is subjective, as most matters of art are. However, if you're trying to make money with your tennis images, or if second-party approval is important to you for some other reason, then you need to consider the subjective opinion of others. That opinion tends to change with time and place. Whether cutoffs are acceptable is affected by trends and by the opinions of the current set of art directors and photo editors who make decisions about which photos get used and which do not.

Still, best practice is to follow at least one rule that does tend to persevere: Never cut off a limb at a joint. In other words, don't allow the edge of the frame to cut through an ankle, a knee, an elbow or a shoulder. The result just looks awkward.

Aside from that, your preference is your rule. My preference is to keep my photos in one of four groups:

Full-body photos tend to be best for instruction (because you can see the player's entire form and mechanics) and for especially athletic shots (such as jumping or running).

FULL-BODY

Every body part is included in the frame, including both feet and both legs, both hands and both arms, and, it should go without saying, the head. Some would argue that the racquet, compositionally speaking, is an extension of the arm, and therefore should also be included. As hard as that can sometimes be, I tend to agree, at least for the purpose of a full-body shot—missing the racquet can steal from the "completeness" of the player. The racquet head is important; for best results, keep at least half of it in the frame.

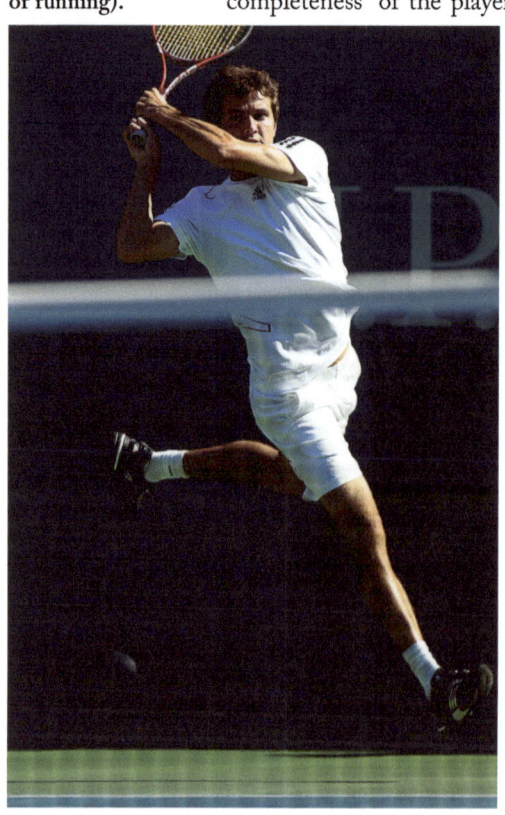

When shooting a full-body photo, you usually will want to frame the player so that he or she fills the composition. Doing so, however, creates a problem: Because players move, it becomes very easy for their heads to unexpectedly pop above the top of the frame. Therefore, you'll find yourself paying close attention to avoid that, which then makes it very easy for their feet to slip off the bottom of the frame. If you don't pay attention to both the top and bottom of the player's body, I promise that you'll be severing appendages at a frustrating pace. The solution is to try waiting for the player to set his or her stance before hitting the ball. The moment will be fleeting, but there is usually an instant when the feet will be planted before the player starts moving the racquet forward. At that instant, ensure the feet are in your frame, then quickly move your eye up to check the head and see the action. Then you can time your shot knowing that the player's whole body is in the composition. This can be challenging—it requires quick reactions—but is often the difference between trash and treasure. (You could also frame loose and crop later.)

HALF-BODY

The trouble with full-body framing is that it often leaves dead space at the sides of the photo. A person's body just does not fill the 2-to-3 proportions of a standard photograph well. (Perhaps a sumo wrestler's body would, but not a tennis player's.) With experience and thought, you can learn to use that cushion creatively as negative space (when it's possible). Or you can concentrate your camera's view closer to the action to eliminate the dead space—but then, of course, you'll have to cut off part of the player's body.

I usually find it awkward to crop anywhere along the legs—not for philosophical reasons, but because it tends to throw the frame's "weight" off-balance. Cropping near the waist is better, because it's the natural mid-point to the human form. Showing all of the top half along with just some of the bottom half usually just ends

Half-body framing tends to be best for capturing dynamic action and exciting (perhaps "cover-worthy") photos.

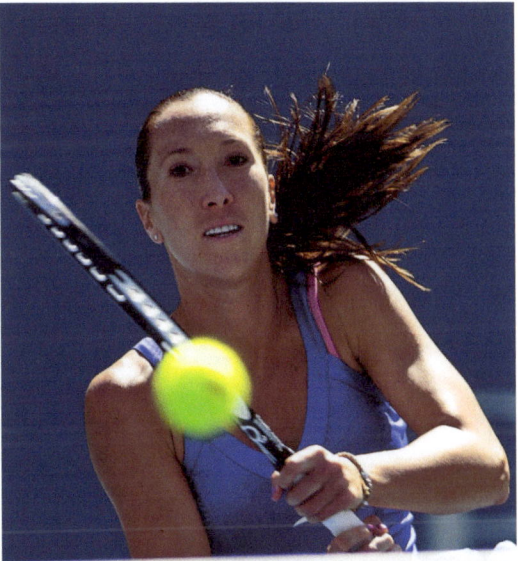

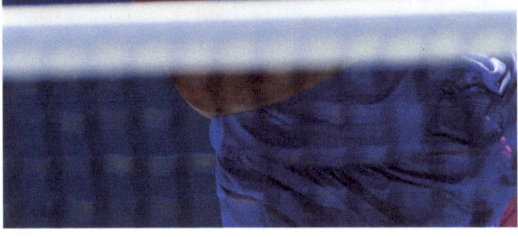

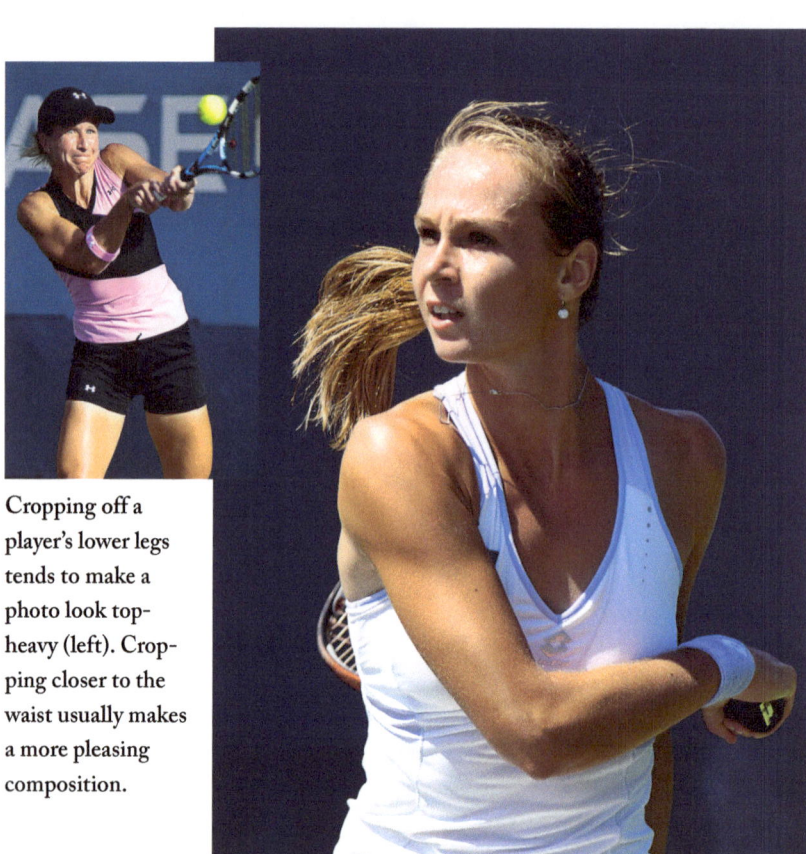

Cropping off a player's lower legs tends to make a photo look top-heavy (left). Cropping closer to the waist usually makes a more pleasing composition.

up looking wrong. So instead, use the waist (or thereabouts) as the cut-off. Including just the upper half of the body allows you to fill the frame, and also generally puts the player's eyes (which, along with the ball, is one of the two key focal points in a tennis photo) right along a rule-of-thirds line.

EXTREME CLOSE-UP

This is when you get relatively close to the player and shoot with a telephoto lens. The aim is to fill the composition with just the face and shoulders, along with the ball and the racquet, at the millisecond that they're all in your very tight frame.

This is difficult to accomplish. It's so difficult, in fact, that you'll likely feel a bit crazy for even attempting it. Timing the shutter release is almost a guess—an educated guess, but a gamble nonetheless. It's also a low-yield approach to tennis photography. You'll generate a lot of junk and your delete button could suffer some wear. The good shots, though, will tend to be among your best photos. You'll have to make a lot of exposures to get there, but don't worry—one match will give you literally hundreds of opportunities.

Zeroing in this close to the player means it's nearly impossible to keep elbows or entire arms in the composition. That's okay. The subject is mostly about the player's expression and the moment of impact (or near-impact) with the ball. In this case, what's important to keep in the frame is the eyes, the racquet and the ball. In order to do that, you'll usually need to be situated lower than the action (see "Getting Low," below).

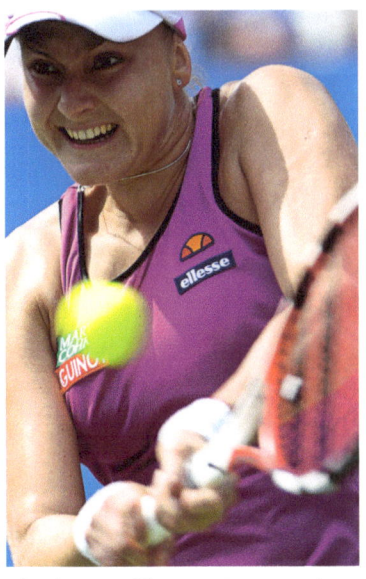

Extreme close-ups are best for an "action profile," for showing facial expressions during play, and for creating "wow-factor" images.

This is a time when chimping (a somewhat derogatory term for checking your photos on your camera's LCD during the shoot) is not only okay, but nearly necessary. Making this kind of photo is easier to accomplish than it was in the film days, because the digital camera's LCD will reveal how you need to tweak your timing. When shooting this tight to

Getting Low

Most players tend to hit the ball around waist level. So if your camera is at the same height as the player, and therefore aimed on a plane parallel to the ground, shooting an extreme close-up will get you only the player's face, not the ball (which will be below the frame). Moreover, the player will be looking down out of the picture.

However, if you get lower than the player (almost at ground-level), you can shoot up at an angle that will align the low ball with the high face. This position is easier to obtain if shooting from a recessed photo pit such as those found at some pro-tennis venues. It is not otherwise impossible, just uncomfortable: Try to sit, kneel or lie on the ground where you can shoot up at the player. (Note that this may be acceptable only in a casual tennis atmosphere.)

the action, being a fraction of a second off is the difference between a great image and junk. Two fractions of a second off means you didn't get the ball, and probably not the racquet, either. Three fractions of a second and your photo won't even include the player. So use that LCD.

Lastly, I find that making extreme close-ups of the action works best from the backhand side, where the player's mechanics are usually more compact. Forehands are rarely hit two-handed, and the non-racquet arm angles out from the body. Due to the nature of tight framing, cropping out that arm in a pleasing way tends to be nearly impossible.

Environmental framing is best for showing a scene or to emphasize the relationship between the tennis and where it's being played. This approach is very photojournalistic. How much of a story can you tell in one image?

ENVIRONMENTAL

A style of wildlife photography and portraiture that has become popular is to show not only the subject, but the subject *in its environment*. The image is of an entire scene that is more than just a bear or an engineer, but of a bear's life in a Yellowstone forest, or of an engineer overseeing the construction of some new technology.

This same technique can be put to use in sports photography. Done well, the background becomes just as important as the game. You're showing the player in a tennis-playing atmosphere, amongst the fans or the facility or the other courts.

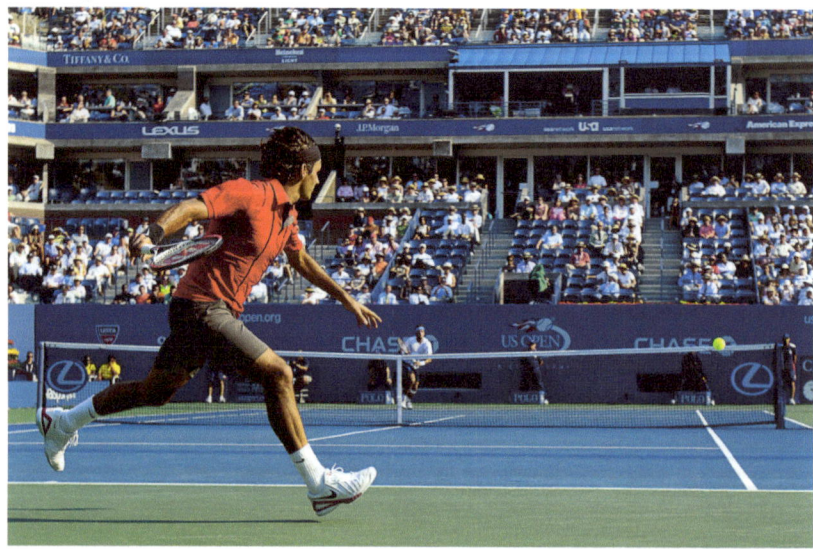

This type of photo is usually made with a normal or wide-angle lens, such as a 60mm or 24mm. Therefore, the player (or players, if you're shooting from behind the court) often appear smaller in the frame than usual. With this strategy, you need to take particular care with composition, placing the player(s) and key background elements in aesthetically pleasing places in the image. As with any wide-angle photo, the rules of composition become more difficult to control and therefore more important *to* control.

Also, light becomes an especially important element with environmental framing. The best approach is to think of the scene as a landscape, and then to photograph it much the same. Control the light and shadows so that they interplay to create a striking image. The tennis component does not overtake this priority, but rather adds to it to create something that might be unexpected for the viewer.

Dealing With Movement

No matter how you decide to frame your action photos, one constant will always affect you: The player *will* move. What does this mean for the tennis photographer? You have to constantly be ready to adjust your framing.

The most obvious example is when a player is running. They're moving, so of course you need to follow with your camera. Based on where he or she moves on court, you may need to zoom in or out, or try switching from vertical to horizontal, constantly adjusting your composition to be ready to record a good photo when it happens.

However, when the player stops running, you can't stop adjusting. Why? Because the player will still be moving. Although the feet are set, the hips are moving, the shoulders are moving, the arms are moving, the hands are moving. Muscle tension will change, posture will change, eye-level will change. All these movements will alter the dynamic of the composition—if you set your framing too early, your photo won't be what you expect. And if you're framed tightly, the player may even move right out of the photo.

The degree to which these changes happen will be different from player to player and from shot to shot. As the photographer, you want to keep these possibilities in your mind, and you need to be ready to adapt to them. If you don't, you will find that keeping the player framed the way you want is nearly impossible. The effect is usually that a body part flies out of the frame: a head, an arm, a leg. Any or all of them can move in the split second before the ball is hit. The good news is that if you're conscious of this, you can predict the movement.

This comes into play in every direction. Players are moving left to right all the time, so they will always be moving across your frame horizontally. If you stop following the movement too early, the player will run out of your composition.

This issue will also affect you vertically. Most players will crouch a little in the back-swing, and then move up again when they bring the racquet forward. Subsequently, they will move up in your frame. If you don't compensate for this, you'll end up cutting off the player's head. So if you notice a particular player does this routinely, you'll want to frame the image with extra room at the top; when the player rises to hit the ball, he or she will rise into the space you left.

The player might also move in other ways. Some rise when they hit, some sink, some stay still—players with undisciplined mechanics may do all three. (That sounds impossible, but I assure you that I've seen it.) Additionally, a player will likely move one way when hitting with topspin

When running, players' arms and legs can fly out of a tight composition (left). When hitting from a set position, a player will often rise out of a crouch—if you don't compensate, he or she may rise right out of your frame (right).

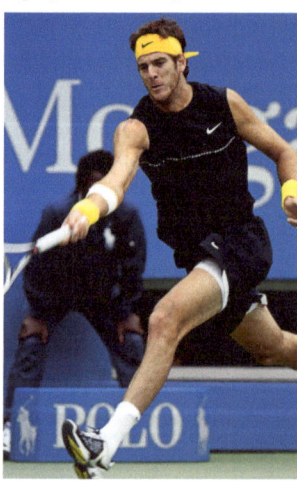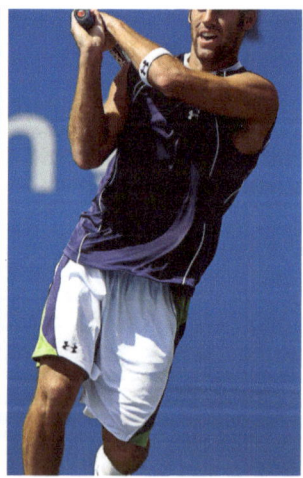

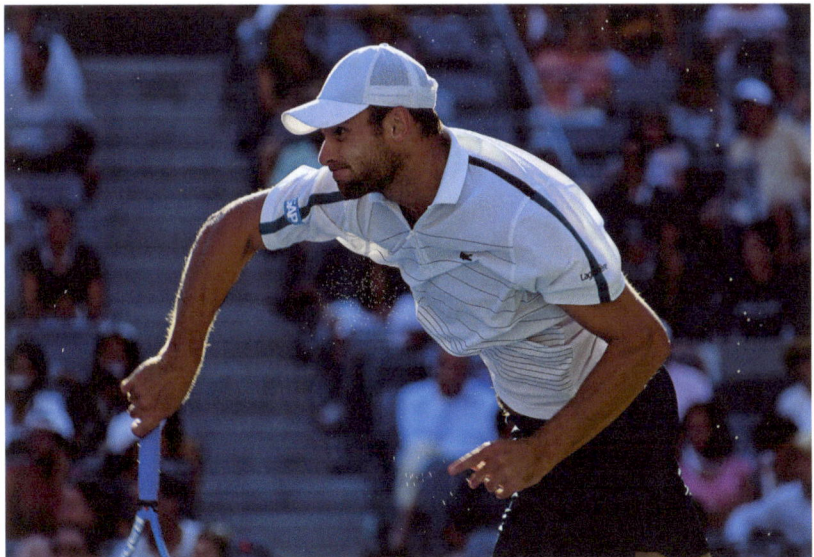

and another when hitting with backspin. If a player has to run and reach for a wide shot, his or her body will almost always drop toward the ground; this means you need to simultaneously track horizontally *and* be prepared to compensate vertically.

I don't mean to make this sound like a complicated problem to deal with. It's not. It's just an issue that might not be initially obvious, yet it *will* affect your photography. You can adjust in two ways:

1. Keenly watch for changes in body movement, and then wait for and react to them.

2. Anticipate the changes and preemptively move the camera to prepare.

The former strategy is best for beginners; the latter is best once you've learned the varyied nuances of different players.

If you find it hard to adjust—if, for example, you keep losing a player's arm despite your best efforts to compensate with framing and timing—then you may be shooting from the wrong angle. So look for a different spot to shoot from. The answer may be to move more to the player's side so you can better line up his or her errant body parts. If you

The serve follow-through is a great example of a shot that requires setting your frame and letting the player move (in this case, fall) into it.

think through how that player's body looks when hitting the ball, you can probably visualize how to orient yourself. Be cognizant of where the problem limbs are at the moment of impact with the ball, then move (while minding etiquette) to an angle that will allow you to keep everything framed nicely (again, see Figure 6 on page 51).

Framing the Ball

Controlling where the player and racquet fall in the frame is not the only composition skill the tennis photographer needs to master. The object of the entire game revolves around that fuzzy yellow ball, so then much of your action photos will, too.

While timing your photos to include the ball can be challenging (see Chapter 6), you also need to deal with the issue of where the ball will be in the frame. Most beginners don't think about this—they just assume that if the ball is

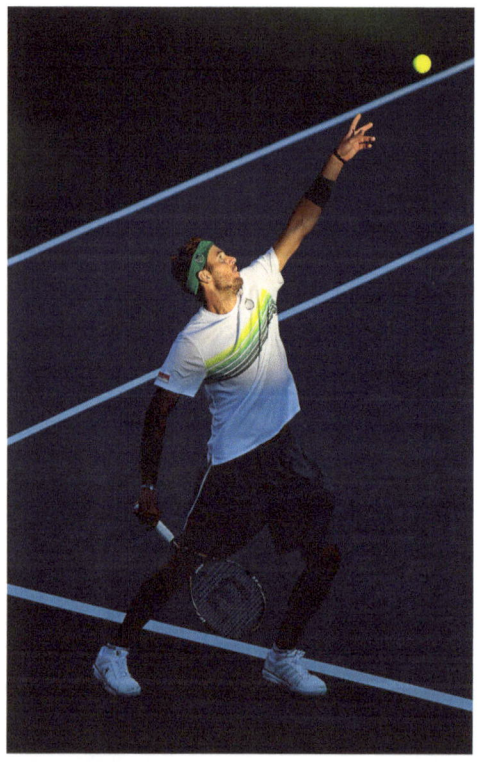

in the image, then they got the shot. But consider how much better a tennis photo can be if you learn to control *where* the ball is in the composition.

You could choose not to worry about this and just hope for the best, and that is probably a good strategy if you're learning the basics of shooting the sport. But eventually you may want to master the technique of controlling the ball. Otherwise you'll likely end up with a lot of photos where it just ends up in some random spot of the frame (on the ground, for example) where, because it's yellow, it actually draws the viewer's eye away from the player and therefore becomes a hindrance to a truly successful photograph.

> Try to capture the ball in a compositionally sound spot. Here, it's the point of highest contrast, and the sideline, the lines in the shirt, the player's arm and his line of sight all lead right to it.

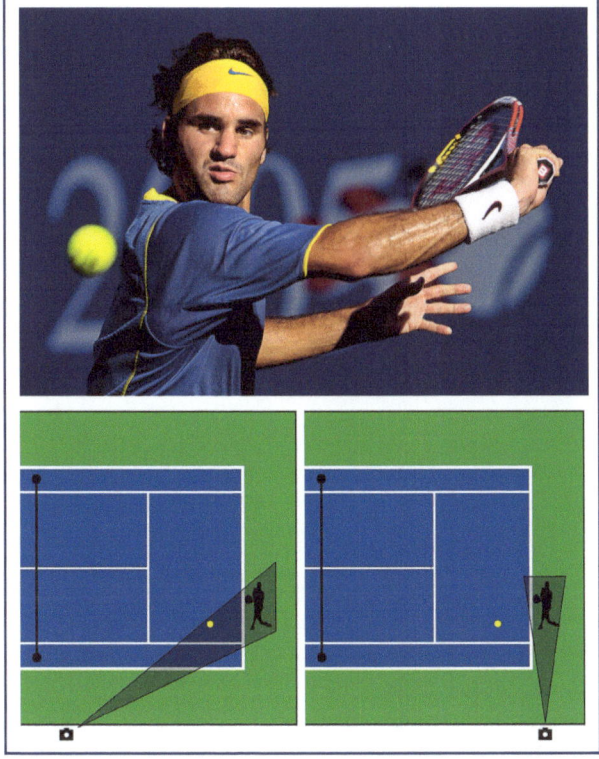

Figure 15
In order to line up a high ball with a player's shoulder, you probably want to be at about a 45-degree angle (bottom left). If you were shooting from 90 degrees, a ball at that height usually wouldn't be in your frame yet (bottom right).

As with so many aspects of tennis photography, your strategy for composing the ball is usually related to your angle. Think about where the ball will be in your field of view, and how that relates to what the player will be doing at the instant they're in your frame at the same time.

For example, if you want to frame the ball in front of the player's shoulder, you'll probably need to open the shutter at the high spot of the bounce — because there are few other times when the ball will be that high. (This assumes that the player is not hitting the ball low and on the rise, in which case the ball would never get that high.) Therefore, you cannot position yourself at a 90-degree angle to the action, because at that moment the ball would still be about 10 feet from the player, and subsequently too far outside your frame. By the time the ball entered your view, it would already have dropped to waist level. So instead you would need to find an angle that allows you to align the player and the ball when it's at the high-point of its arc (see Figure 15).

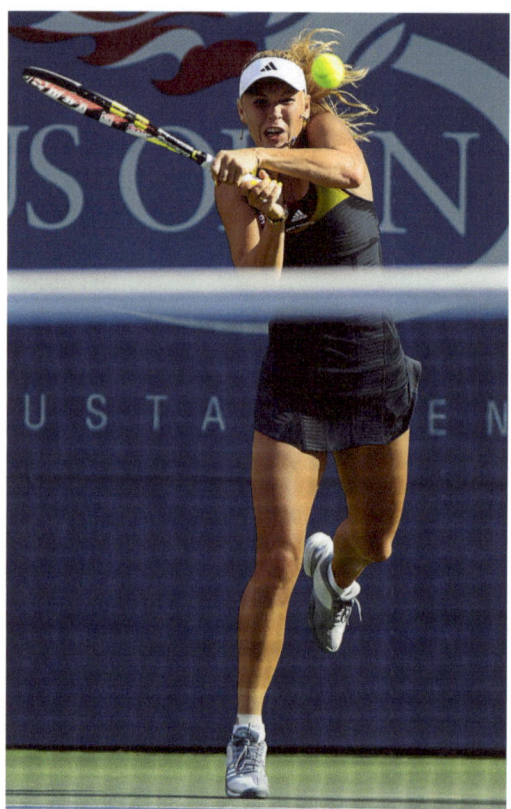

Another example could entail exactly the opposite scenario. If you want to frame the ball at waist level, that opportunity will most likely exist at or near the point of impact with the racquet. You could also do this from a 45-degree angle, but that's probably not best. Think about the swing mechanics of a player at that moment—shoulders tense, head looking down—and you'll realize that more often than not it won't be a pretty picture. However, at the 90-degree angle, the player will be looking into the frame, and the scrunched parts of the body won't look as awkward. Moreover, the ball will probably fall into a

The easiest way to capture the ball after impact is to position yourself at a zero-degree angle from the action, shooting from behind the court and looking across the net.

more compositionally pleasing spot, even possibly along a line of thirds.

Once again, all of these specifics vary from player to player, and learning their tendencies will help you decide how to capture the ball in the frame almost exactly where you want it. There's no one rule to follow—you just need to be aware of the concept that you *can* control where the ball will fall in the composition based on your angle to the action, and then practice doing so.

Try this exercise (similar to the one in Chapter 3, but with a further motive): Move around the edges of the court, all the while focusing on one player. Try to get the player and the ball in the frame together from every angle. (For now, don't worry about whether the photo looks good.) You'll see how your position affects when you can align the two, which will then dictate at what point you can photograph the action (with the ball) from that spot. And that, by extension, will dictate where you can place the ball in the frame. The concept is simple, but admittedly complex to describe and challenging to execute.

A few guidelines may help:

1. If you want to capture the ball at impact, just frame the player well and you'll probably get the ball in a nice spot.

2. If you want to capture the ball before impact, determine (based on your angle) where in the composition you need to leave room for the ball, then anticipate how and when it will arrive there. (This will become easier with practice and experience.)

3. If you want to capture the ball after impact, you'll need to be at a very slight angle to the action, or perhaps no angle at all (in other words, shooting from the backcourt). From a wider angle, the ball will usually be moving too fast off the racquet to time a shot successfully. But if you're shooting from the end of the court and the ball is hit right toward you, you'll have plenty of opportunity to frame it well.

Remember that just because the ball is in the frame does not mean you've made a good photograph. If the location of the ball hurts the composition, be brave and hit delete.

Oops Moments

When you're in the midst of shooting hundreds of frames that require quick reactions and split-second decisions, you are destined to make some images that appear, to put it euphemistically, imprudent. The two most common inadvertent offenses are:

1. When a female player wearing a tennis skirt strikes the ball, the skirt will tend to fly up when

her hips turn. Sometimes the result is elegant, perhaps even "ballerina-like," as my tennis-photographer friend Michael Cole once said. But more often, because her legs are positioned wide apart while hitting, the result is inelegant and unladylike.

2. When a male player prepares to hit a first serve, he generally puts an extra ball in his shorts pocket. During running and hitting, that ball will move about. If it drops between his legs at the moment you open your shutter, the result is an image of his shorts bulging.

Boys may find these images funny, and some disreputable tabloids may like to print such accidents. Other than those two exceptions, few people want to see these photos, and fewer people will want to buy, publish or otherwise use them. These images don't even make it onto my computer—I delete them in-camera.

Women in Action

Another issue is how a female player's expression may look during on-court action.

Most athletes, when they torque their body and release all their strength into a ball coming at them at 100-plus miles per hour, tend to distort their face. They grimace, they snarl, they scrunch, and so on. Due to what many would call a double-standard, some people accept these expressions on men but not on women. The notion seems to be that the male athlete should look strong and warrior-like, while the female athlete should just look pretty.

Monica Seles is a perfect example of a woman with this issue. In my first job at Tennis magazine, part of my charge was to maintain the massive library of photographs from our contracted and staff photographers. Of the thousands of Seles photos in the files, there were *three* in which her face was not scrunched up mid-swing. I was responsible for always knowing the location of those three slides.

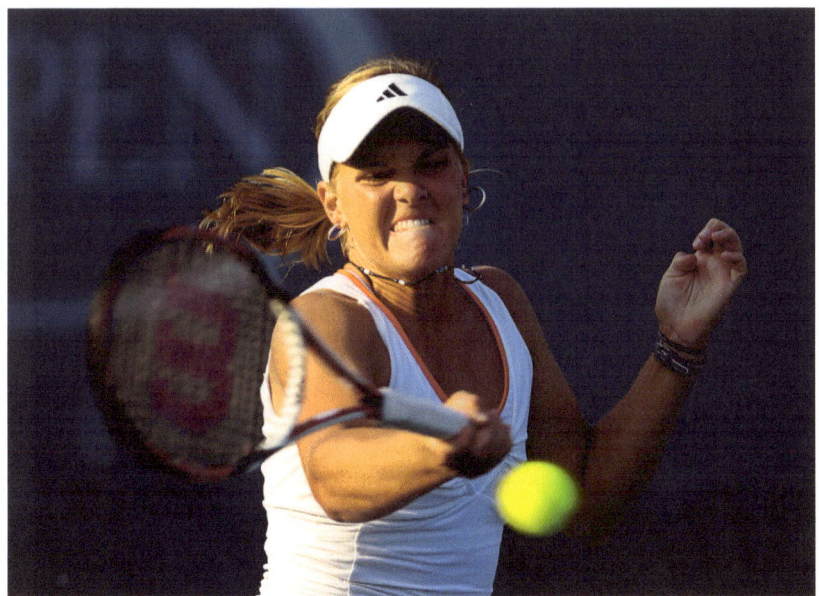

My opinion is that this shouldn't even be a concern. Maybe it's because I grew up when the gender-equality issue was already mainstream, but I feel that an athlete is an athlete, and when she hits the ball, she looks how she looks. However, I just make the photos, I don't buy them. If you're licensing images, then the buyer's opinion may matter most. Some people agree with me, some don't, and that's fine. But it's a difference of opinion that's worth being aware of.

I don't agree that appearing intense and athletic detracts from beauty. But it's prudent to know that some paying clients may feel otherwise.

FOCUS

A critical part of composition is focus. It helps direct the viewer's attention, and at its best is often the difference between expert and mediocre imagery.

I hate to say there are "rules" in photography, but here's one that applies to 99.9 percent of tennis images: You want your sharpest focus to be the player's eyes. As with all rules, you can break this one for creative purposes, but if you're doing any sort of straight-forward action photo wherein the important subject is the person playing, then his or her eyes should be tack sharp.

For this reason, whether shooting horizontal or vertical format, you will usually want to auto-focus using a sensor along the top line of the rule of thirds (assuming your camera has multiple focus sensors, as discussed in Chapter 2). This allows you to focus on the eyes while maintaining a fundamentally sound composition (see Figure 2 on page 16). If you're just starting out in sports photography, practice this technique, even to the detriment of composition. You can always adjust your composition by cropping in post-production, but no software or digital developing techniques can fix bad focus.

I do, however, recommend testing your gear before adhering too strictly to this strategy. In many cameras the accuracy of the autofocus sensors is not uniform—the middle sensor tends to produce the sharpest results. Do some test photos to determine if any of your sensors result in soft focus. If so, either avoid using those sensors, get a new camera, or use a smaller aperture so that the depth of field will mask the deficiency.

If your camera has only one autofocus sensor, or only one that you trust, a common method of compensating is to point the sensor at your target, lock the focus (most DSLRs have a button for this), then recompose. This technique is actually not best-practice in general photography, as it changes the focal distance and can result in soft images. That problem, however, is not so drastic in tennis. Because you're probably shooting relatively long-range, the change in distance is tiny, percentage-wise—so you really wouldn't perceive the difference.

Points on Focus

Two technical matters can affect how you use autofocus when shooting tennis. First, if your camera was made anytime recently, it will likely feature a multi-point autofocus system. But beware when shooting tennis. Multi-point focusing is almost always slower than single-sensor. For best results, use one autofocus sensor to track a player, and choose a sensor along a rule-of-thirds line.

Second, autofocus sensors are usually quicker when the lens is already close to being in focus. Therefore, to speed things up during the action, pre-focus on your subject before play starts.

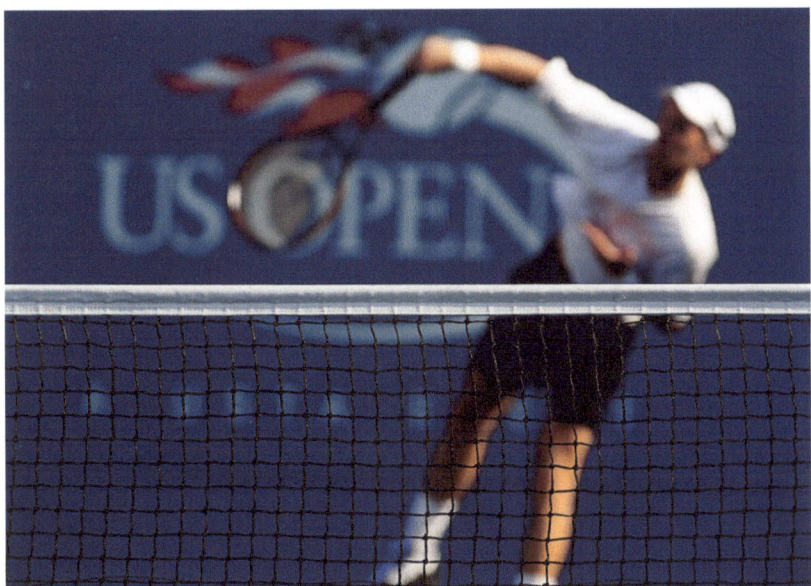

However, the problem you *will* face is that this technique is nearly impossible to accomplish while following a moving target. If you are able to manage focusing, locking and recomposing before you miss the shot, you'll just have to repeat the whole process as soon as the player moves again. You could just get another camera. Or you could shoot with a smaller aperture (f/5.6, at minimum) to increase your depth of field. (However, this will make your background more distinct, and will make achieving fast shutter speeds more difficult.)

For creative purposes, you can break the rule that advises always keeping the player as the sharpest focus in the photo.

Finish Focusing

Once you're happy with how your camera is focusing, let it finish its job. During a fast pace of tennis action, sometimes you will see a great photo opportunity happening in front of you quickly, and you may be tempted to fire the shutter before your autofocus is set. Don't. Not only will you end up with a photo that you'll have to throw away, but you will also miss the great photo that might occur a fraction of a second later when the camera *would* be in focus. Missing great chances can be painful, but haste can double that disappointment.

A strategy for defeating that temptation is to lock your camera so that the shutter will open only if the lens is properly focused. (Most DSLRs have a setting for this.) I did this for a few years, but eventually backed off the idea. I was indeed saved from bunches of out-of-focus photos, but I also know for sure that I missed shots that would have been good — perhaps the aperture was small enough to compensate for the slightly soft focus, or maybe the moment was more important than the technical perfection of the image. Whatever the reason, I eventually concluded that I always want my camera to do what I tell it, no matter what. I would rather have to cope with mistakes than missed opportunities.

Stolen Focus

Another technical obstacle with autofocus arises from how the sensors work. They're actually a little bigger than the tiny indicator you see in the viewfinder. Combine that with

Killer Blobs

An important rule of composition revolves around the idea of a photo's "point of highest contrast" — the spot in the image where the brightest bright juts against the darkest dark. That's the spot where the viewer's eye is usually drawn first. Therefore, a photographer cognizant of this generally ensures that the point of highest contrast resides in an important element of the composition, so as not to detract from the subject. That's why a bright, out-of-focus blob in the background is usually undesirable — because it steals the viewer's attention from the player. And bright blobs are pretty common in tennis environments, especially in the

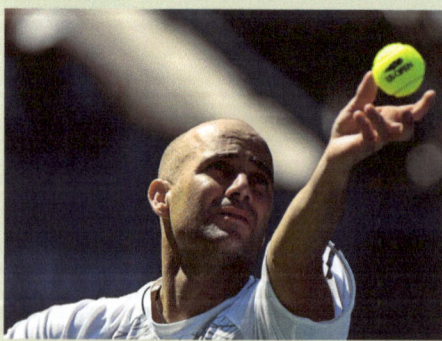

stands of organized tournaments. However, the fix is usually easy: By shifting the camera just a few inches in any direction, you can move that blob out of the background. Another choice is to use the blob creatively — if you can move it behind the player's head, for example, then that could make him or her stand out even more.

the fact that autofocus thrives on high-contrast objects, and you see a problem arise with tennis: A racquet, with its tight weave of taut strings, is about the most high-contrast object you could put in a scene. And the sensors *love* it.

Especially if you're using a camera with dynamic autofocus (wherein the focus follows the subject, rather than staying strictly on the sensor you activate), a racquet sweeping through the frame can readily steal your lens' attention. You probably won't even notice that it happened until you review your photos on a large monitor later.

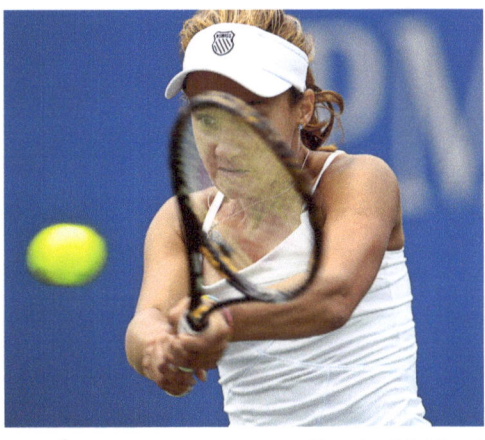

Depth of field and motion blur made this photo possible. Without them, you wouldn't be able to see the player's face through the racquet.

The solution? If you have a dynamic autofocus setting that seems to create more problems than it solves, just shut it off. Otherwise, these problems can be difficult to avoid. Just know that they won't interfere terribly often — they won't ruin every photograph you try to make. You do your best to bypass the quirks of the technology, and you accept that sometimes you'll have to throw away what could have been a good photo. You still will most likely end up with many more sharp images than if you had focused manually.

DEPTH OF FIELD

In tennis photography, shallow depth of field is almost always your friend. Look around any tennis environment. The background is filled with distracting elements: fences, nets, other courts, stands full of fans. All of them are easier to work with when your aperture is large.

If you're shooting any tennis match with an audience, whether a pro or amateur event, you will probably be shooting from the side of the court. As discussed in Chapter 3, if you therefore try to keep the crowd out of the background of your photo, you will sacrifice a large percentage of your court coverage (see Figure 7 on page 57). However, if you want to allow the crowd in, you probably don't want it to

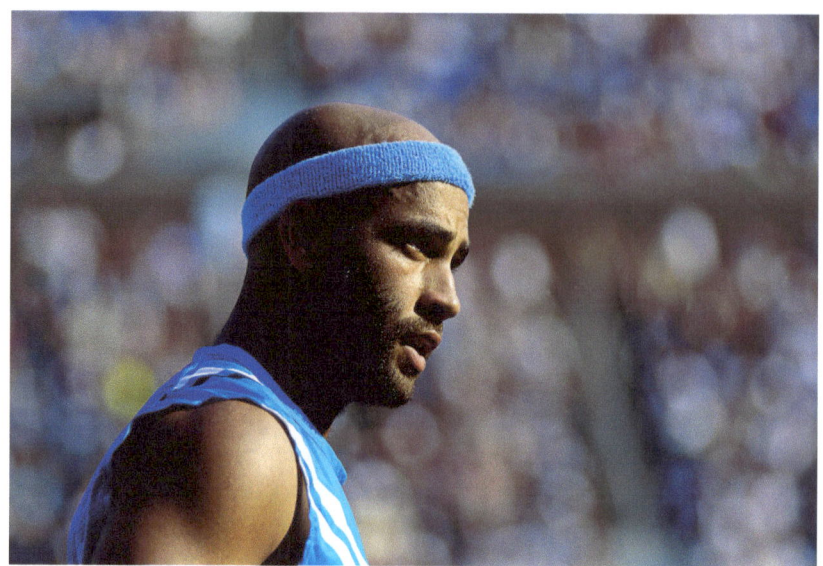

A large aperture and the resulting shallow depth of field can obscure a busy crowd into a pleasantly soft background.

be in sharp focus—there is just way too much detail for it not to become a compositional problem.

You can often resolve that issue with shallow depth of field. In fact, if you can make the crowd focus soft enough, you can create a nice abstract pattern in the background of your image. Accomplishing this will require one of two things. The most obvious is using a large aperture—f/2.8 is ideal among the most accessible options (see the section on lens choice in Chapter 2). You can find lenses with wider apertures, but they will be too short for most tennis applications. Nikon and Canon each make a topnotch 200mm f/2, but that focal length has limited applications. It's more useful in casual tennis environments than in pro tournaments. Alternatively, when coupled with a sensor smaller than 35mm (such as an APS-C sensor), the magnification factor can turn those lenses into a 300mm f/2 or a 400mm f/2, which can be incredibly useful for softening a busy background (though this is offset somewhat by the fact that smaller formats happen to produce greater depth of field).

However, that's a fixed-length option. The zoom options are limited. Olympus makes a 35-100mm f/2, which on its E-series cameras is effectively a 70-200mm f/2. That's a nice focal length for shooting players who are relatively close to you (such as in a casual setting).

The second option is less obvious, but also less useful in tennis: extension tubes. These accessories allow lenses to focus closer than they were designed to, in order to facilitate macro photography with non-macro gear (or to make macro lenses *more* macro). However, another effective use for tubes is to decrease depth of field. The combination of an extension tube and a long lens can soften a background quite nicely.

Unfortunately, this is not a cure-all for depth-of-field issues in tennis because tubes also limit how *far* you can focus a lens. For example, rather than being able to focus to infinity, a 300mm lens coupled with an extension tube will focus to a maximum of only about 12 feet away (depending on the size of the tube). That's not close enough for most tennis-photography situations. Still, I always encourage experimenting. If you have tubes, try using them on court — see what you can do with them in the tennis environment. When shooting pro matches, the only time I've been able to make this technique work effectively is when shooting a player waiting to return a serve — right in front of me.

A word of warning, however, when throwing the crowd this much out of focus: Watch for blobs. Human perception adapts well to the limitations of our eyes. Our subconscious mind constructs a focused image from unfocused input. So while our eyes may not be focused on the crowd, in the viewfinder we still passively perceive it to be in focus. Therefore,

---

Selective Focus

Though you can use greater depth of field to get the player's face, the ball and the racquet all in focus at once, don't feel you need to accomplish that goal. If a wider range of focus is important to you, then go ahead and aim for that. But thinner, selective focus will usually not detract from the action. If the ball is in a

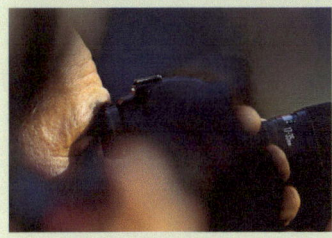

good place in the composition, and the racquet is a little blurry (either because of focus or motion), then the story of the action is complete — sharply focused or not. In fact, leaving the ball and racquet slightly soft can help isolate the most important aspect of your photo: the player.

we are sometimes surprised at an image the camera records. In the case of an out-of-focus crowd, this means that any areas of similar colors side-by-side may blend together to form a large blob in the background. If that blob is white or yellow or otherwise brighter than the average tone of the photograph, it will distract the viewer's attention (see "Killer Blobs" on page 110).

Fortunately, shooting with a telephoto lens means that a minimal change in angle has an exaggerated effect. Adjusting your position by just a couple of inches can move that blob entirely out of the background.

All of this discussion has revolved around shallow depth of field, because that's what generally best serves a tennis photo. Still, I encourage not letting this become so well ingrained that you never close down the aperture. Doing so can improve images in many circumstances. For instance, if you want to ensure that the player's face, the ball and the racquet are all in focus, you'll have to wait a long time for them to all fall within the same thin focal plane. Closing down the aperture to f/5.6 or f/8 (if the light allows) will help increase the frequency of those opportunities.

CHAPTER SIX

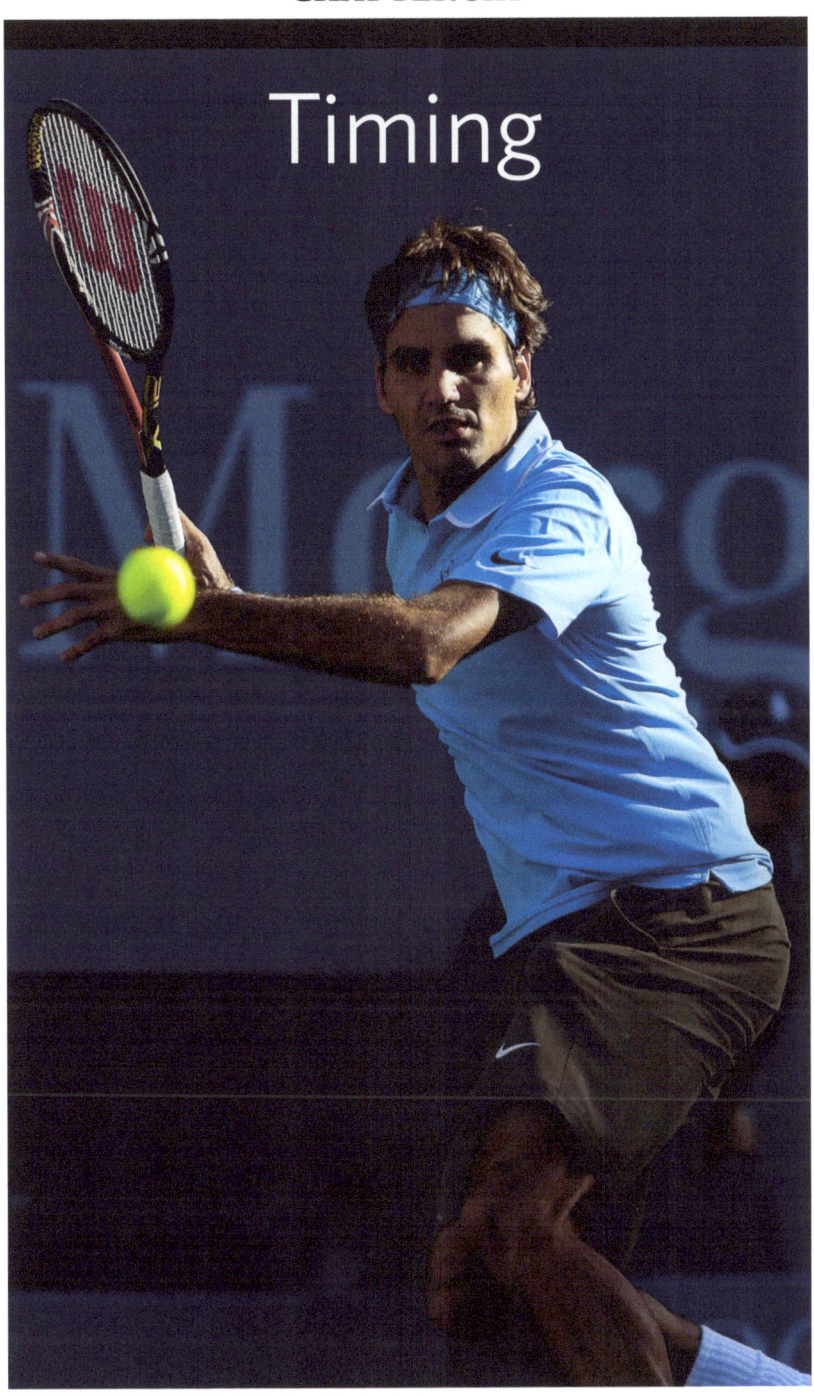

Timing

TIMING

Does a successful action photo need to include the ball? Well, there's a healthy and ongoing debate about that.

The art world is filled with popular pieces that exclude an important element. In fact, the technique is useful in creating a visual mystery or puzzle, in making the viewer think a bit in order to mentally complete the story of the image. No general artistic bias dictates the visual presence of every element of a scene. Therefore, no commonly accepted rule of art, when applied to tennis photography, would mandate a ball's presence in the frame.

Still, many people—including some who make decisions about which photos get used and which don't—feel that the ball is an essential element of a good action shot. This prejudice is born not from art dictate, but rather from the fact that capturing a fast-moving ball in a photo can be hard, and harder still in an especially quick sport such as tennis. Therefore, only a practiced or naturally gifted action photographer can accomplish the feat regularly and at will, especially in a way that improves the composition (see "Framing the Ball" on page 102).

However, taking that rationale too religiously is akin to music aficionados who believe that a song is well written only if it's difficult to play. Not all sans-ball photos are bad. Yes, the ball is an important (even critical) element in some types of tennis images. But not in all. Shots that work well without a ball include ones of follow-throughs, reactions, muscle tension, running, and so on.

Still, even if you don't feel you need to include the ball in every shot, you'll probably want it in at least some. If you're shooting tennis professionally, there's a financial reason: Some clients will insist on having a ball in the photo. And if you're doing this recreationally, there's the impetus of meeting a personal challenge: Trying to capture the ball in flight is fun.

All of this brings us to the issue of timing. You simply cannot, when photographing tennis, wait to see in ball in your viewfinder and then press the shutter release. By the time you react, the ball will be gone. It's just that fast. Instead,

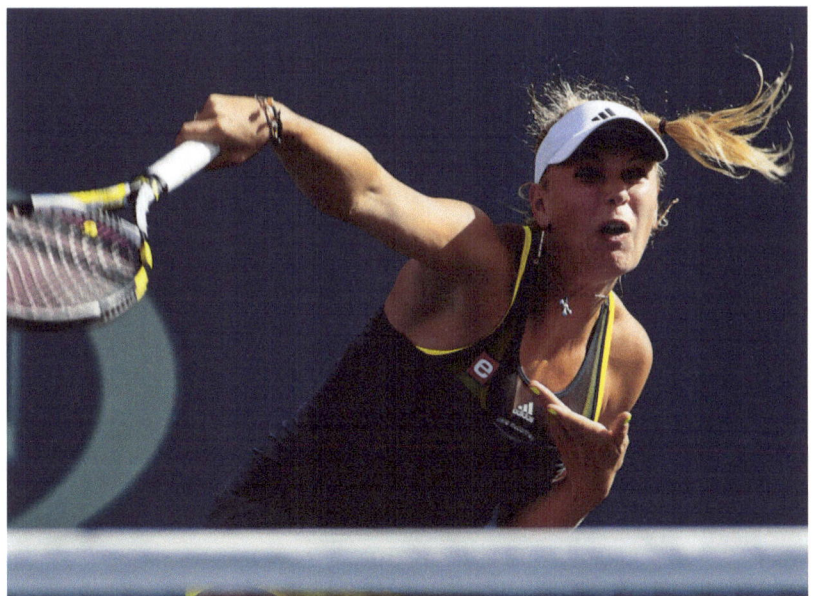

you need to use techniques that will help you anticipate when the ball will be in the frame.

TECHNIQUES

First, some simple advice: The most important thing you can do to make great tennis photos is to know the game. Learn the rules, learn the strategy. Watch matches. Play matches. Talk to tennis fans. An adept understanding of what's happening on court will help you predict the action and anticipate important moments.

Second, a word of warning. None of these techniques are fail-safe. Their rate of success will depend not only on your innate talent or your learned ability to apply them, but also on the idiosyncrasies of different players and specific points. Moreover, a technique that works while photographing one player may fail when photographing another.

These techniques are not a guarantee of precision, but rather a guide to help you develop relatively reliable timing.

SOUND
You can hear the ball. If you have a credential at a pro event, or if you're courtside at an amateur match, then you're closer

Some action photos work just fine without a ball, drawing their energy from other elements of the composition.

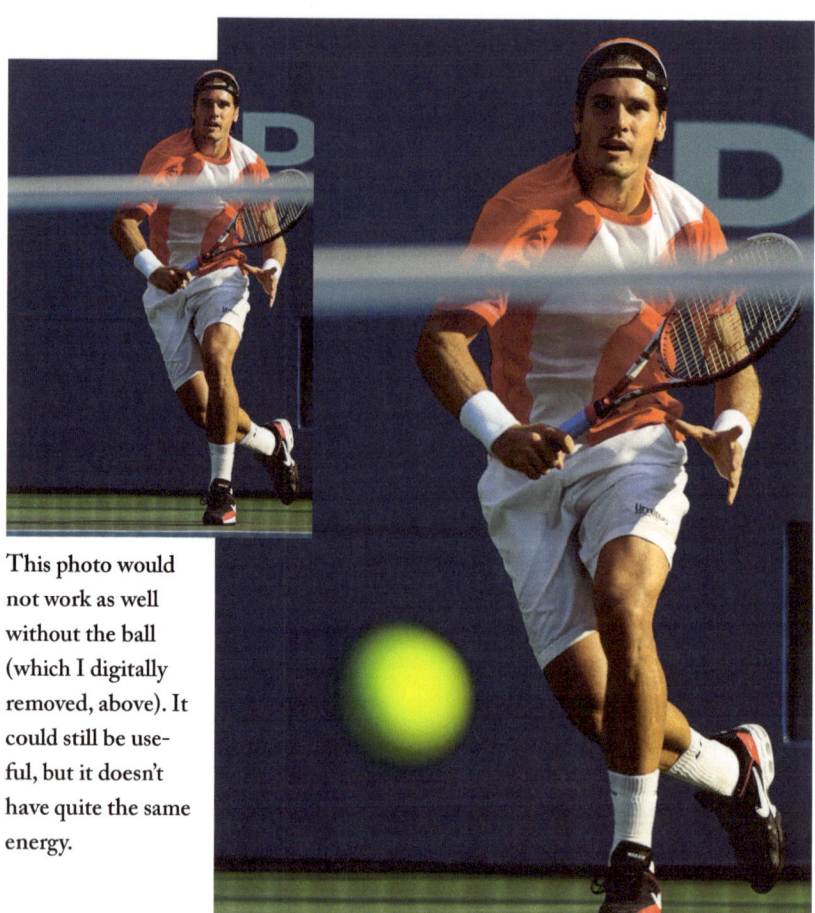

This photo would not work as well without the ball (which I digitally removed, above). It could still be useful, but it doesn't have quite the same energy.

to the action than everyone except the players and officials.

Even if that's not the case, you can hear the ball anyway. Even at the largest tennis arena in the world, the US Open's Arthur Ashe Stadium, you can distinctly hear the thwack of racquet-on-ball from the last row.

You can use that sound to help time your photos. Listen for the rhythm of the ball being hit. It's sometimes variable, due to mixed spins and unusual shots, but most of the time the pattern is relatively consistent. In a long point, especially between two baseliners, being aware of that rhythm can help you predict when the player you're focused on will hit the ball. Anticipate the next thwack in your head, and time your shutter release accordingly.

GROUND SOUND

This technique is more precise, but more difficult, and sometimes impossible.

If the surrounds are quiet enough, instead of listening for the racquet hitting the ball on the other side of the court, listen for the sound of the ball hitting the ground on your side before bouncing up toward the player you're tracking. If you can hear that sound, then wait a fraction of second, and fire. More often than not, you'll capture the ball in the frame.

MUSCLE TWITCH

You have another helpful sensory organ besides your ears: your eyes. As stated before, you can't effectively watch for the ball to come into your composition. However, you can watch for signs that it's about to come.

The one obvious visual signal is how the player is reacting, and lucky for you, he or she is already in your frame. As the ball approaches, the player will prepare to hit. Some back-swings are longer than others—in size and time. But just about every player will in some way twitch right before bringing the racquet forward again to strike the ball.

When a player brings the racquet back, look for the slightest sign that the forward swing is about to begin.

I'm not referring to some secret body language, just the natural movement of muscles that are about to spring into intense action. A few milliseconds after that twitch, the ball will hit the racquet. Every player's timing is a little different, but with a little observation you can learn to coordinate this "tell" with your choice of when

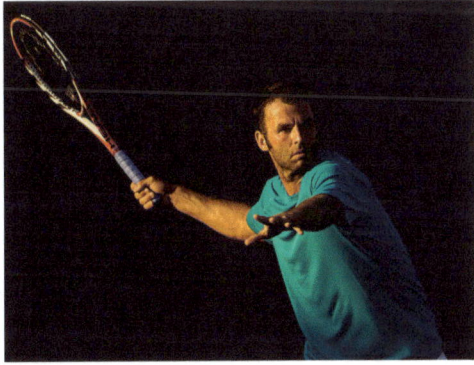

to open the shutter. You are timing your photo not to the ball, but to the player's movement.

The most difficult player to do this with is one who back-swings early and holds still while waiting for the ball, almost like there's a hiccup in his or her mechanics. Even for just that very brief moment, your timing can be fooled. Situations like these are when I misfire most often.

GLIMPSING YELLOW

This is somewhat of an advanced technique, because it requires active use of peripheral vision along with very fast reactions. But with practice, it can be effective.

Frame the player in your viewfinder. Then, keeping the lens on target, turn your attention to the side of the frame where the ball will enter. With your peripheral vision, continue tracking the player while still adjusting your aim to follow his or her movement. In other words, with one eye you're watching two parts of the frame, all within the viewfinder. As soon as you see the tiniest glimpse of yellow at the edge of the frame, fire the shutter.

REDUNDANCY

I advise not relying on any one of the aforementioned techniques. Instead, combine them. An audible cue can help

If you're making any image where the player's form is critical, you'll need to use anticipation techniques for that as well. If you wait until the action looks perfect in your viewfinder, then you've already missed the shot.

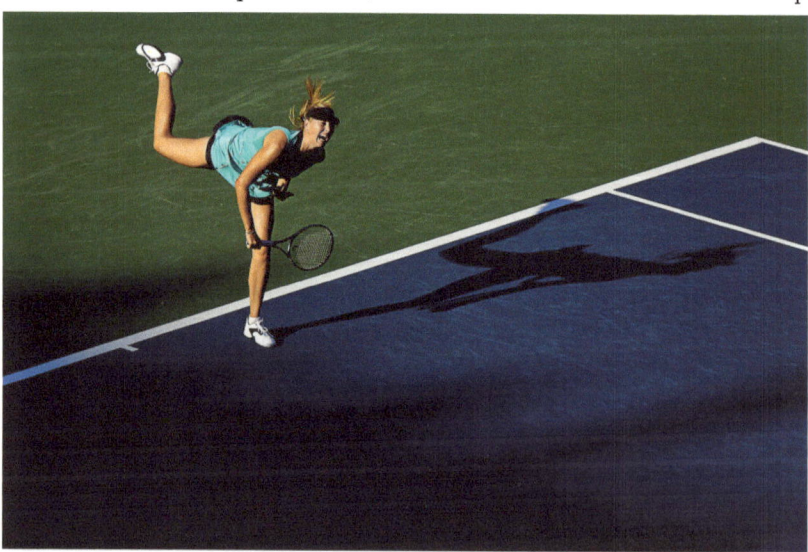

Contact

As if capturing the ball in your frame isn't enough of a challenge, you can also try to capture the ball on the racquet — at contact. This is largely a matter of luck, but trying can be fun. Unfortunately, though, it doesn't often make for a

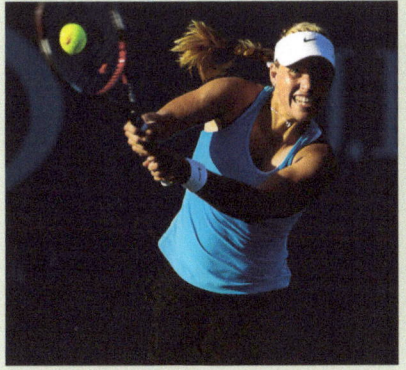

dynamic composition. Also, from a business perspective, it's not very useful. I can recall being asked for a ball-on-racquet photo only once, and that was by a golf magazine. You can also try to freeze the ball immediately after impact, as it's rocketing off the racquet. This is just as challenging (if not more so) because tripping the shutter even the tiniest sliver of a second late means missing the ball completely.

you anticipate a visual cue, or vice versa. Together they give you more data to work with.

Also, a problem with using timing devices is that you can get lulled into over-relying on them and then miss an unusual opportunity. So try not to get so conditioned to shooting at those anticipated moments that you forget to be aware of what's happening between them.

Lastly, remember this: The more you shoot, the more you will develop intuition about when the ball will be in the frame. And that's the ultimate timing tool.

INCONGRUITIES

As with so many aspects of shooting tennis, players' unique quirks can affect your timing decisions.

MECHANICS

As discussed earlier, different players give different tells for when they'll start to swing the racquet. They do other things differently, too. On the serve, the wrist pronates differently, or the arm drops later or earlier. On the follow-through, some players may wrap the racquet arm completely around the neck, while others finish more over the head. Every

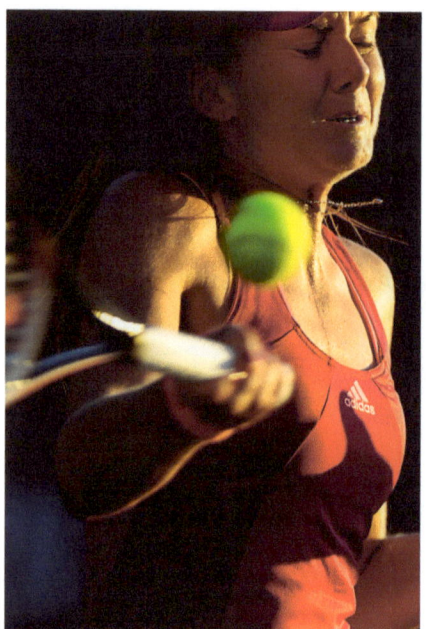

Blinking can ruin what could otherwise have been a great photo.

player hits differently. And these details change not only from player to player, but also from one type of forehand to another.

Taking time to learn a player's mannerisms will help you make more good photos. If you recognize how different players move before, during and after their strokes, you can adjust your timing to make more interesting images.

BLINKING

One of the most troublesome player habits to work around is blinking. Of course, everyone blinks. But some players do it as they're hitting, or immediately after. For the photographer, that's the most inopportune time. If you notice that a player blinks when hitting, you'll want to compensate. Watch in the viewfinder for him or her to re-open their eyes, then shoot a follow-through image. It's not always easy, but it's better than just deleting photos later.

LOOKING DOWN

Another tough task is shooting a player who looks down at a drastic angle while hitting. This is usually a problem with players who hit the ball low. Because they're looking so far down, you can't see their eyes in a photo; if they're wearing a hat, you can't even see any part the face. Additionally, because the ball is so low compared to the body, the only way to get it in the frame is to shoot a vertical, full-body composition, which will end up looking even worse.

Don't even bother trying to shoot these players at impact, because you'll just end up throwing away the photos. Instead, you could try an extreme close-up, as that requires you to get low enough so that the player might be looking a little more toward the camera (see "Getting Low" on page 97). Even that's a gamble, though. Your only calculable solution is to shoot a player like this at follow-through — by that time he or she should be looking up to see where their shot is going, giving you a chance for a nice profile image.

Double-Checking

Timing is a fickle thing. Some days I get the ball in just about every shot—it's like I can't miss, like I've got the best timing of any sports photographer sitting at the edge of any tennis court in the world. Other days you could look at my photos and not know that the match had been played with a ball.

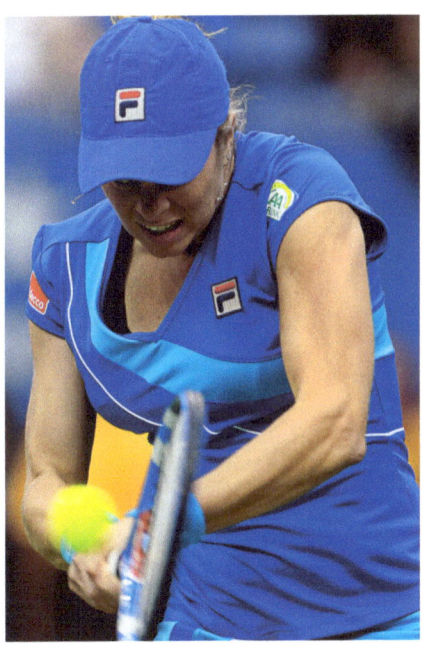

An assortment of issues can throw you off. Had a bad night of sleep? Are you hungry? Overheated? Annoyed? Distracted? All of these can affect you just a smidge, so slightly that you're not even aware that your reactions are diminished. And if you're off by just a little, you could blunder a much higher percentage of good action photos than normal. (Nobody nails every shot.)

Beware the player looking down at impact, especially if he or she is wearing a hat.

This is why chimping is not something to avoid, but something to master doing effectively. Some photographers lecture against reviewing images until later, under the theory that any time you're not looking at your subject is a chance for you to miss a good photo. Yes, that's true. But you risk missing many more good photos by not making sure your timing is as accurate as it might feel.

If for some reason you're lagging a bit, you'll see that on the LCD and can then adjust. Additionally, if you're trying to get a specific image, you'll know when you've successfully made it, and then you can move on to other ideas. (If you have your "blinkies" feature turned on, then chimping also gives you a chance to see if you're blowing out your highlights.) So chimp, and be a better photographer. Just do it intelligently.

CHAPTER SEVEN

Shot Making

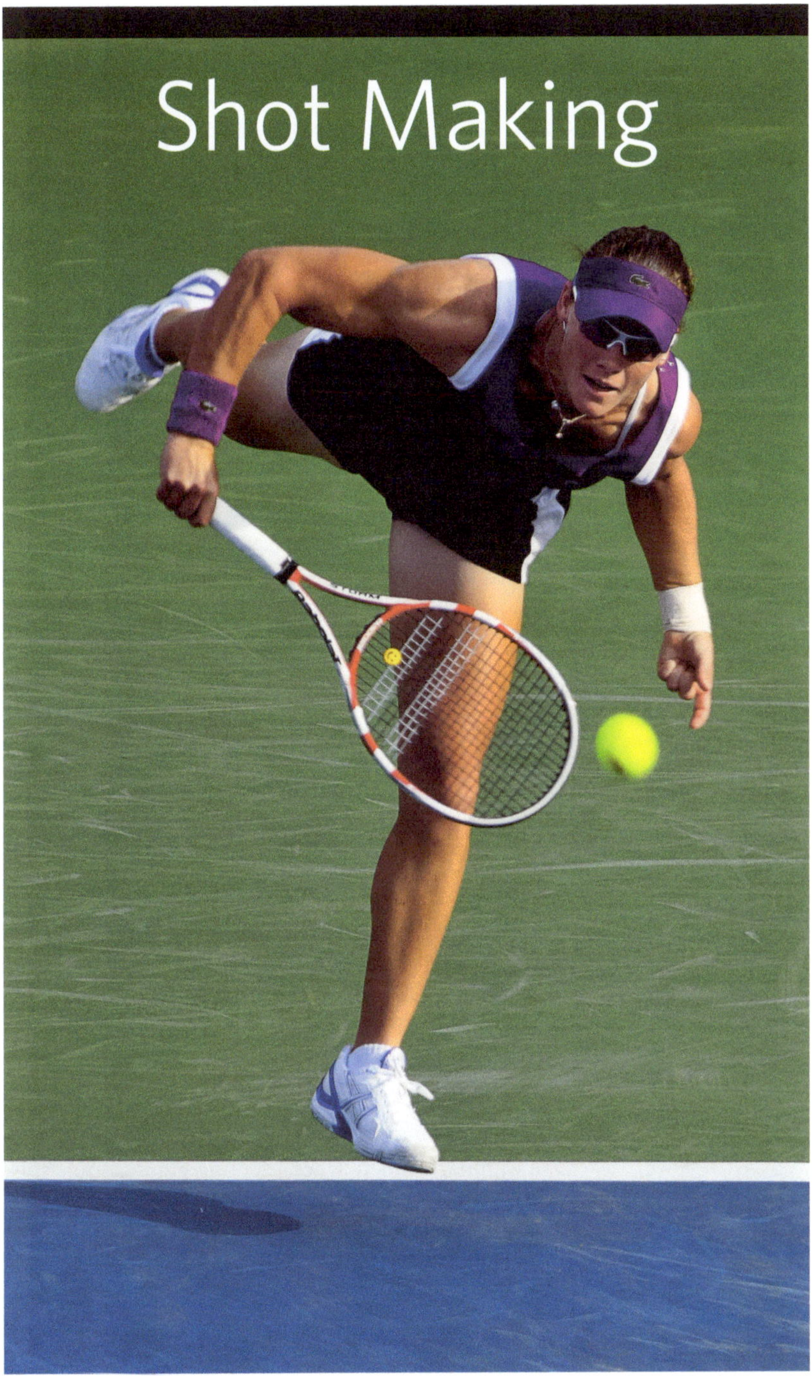

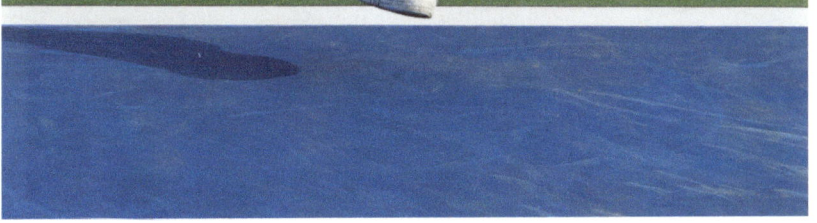

SHOT MAKING

I hesitate to divide tennis photos into categories, because that can limit the imagination. However, for the puropose of demonstration, the following is a breakdown of the "standard" photographs a tennis photographer makes.

Just promise that you'll use this not as a checklist, but as a guide. Be creative. Make something different.

GROUND STROKES

More than half the tennis photos you see and create show forehand and backhand ground strokes, because that's what players spend a majority of each match hitting.

If you want to show the player's mechanics or form, you'll probably want to shoot ground strokes as full-body photos in vertical format. You will perhaps be naturally drawn to shooting verticals anyway, because that's the orientation of the human form. However, I recommend turning to horizontal at least sometimes. Doing so will allow you to frame more tightly and to create more fundamentally solid compositions.

A great ground stroke to shoot is the two-handed backhand. The player will put a lot of energy into the shot, which often translates into an exciting image. Also, the mechanics of the stroke bring both arms in tight to the body, so you won't end up with an errant limb flying out of your photo. And the player will usually hit the ball relatively high, making it easier to include in the composition.

All of that makes the two-handed backhand perhaps the easiest stroke for a photographer to shoot successfully. Because of this, I often start a match by positioning myself to shoot backhands. Doing so helps me adjust my timing quickly, and allows me to feel good about my day sooner.

One warning, though, when shooting ground strokes: If you see the player prepare for a backhand slice, the only way you'll make a good image is if you shoot the back-swing, before the racquet starts to come down. The mechanics of this stroke look awkward in a photograph, because all the player's momentum and focus are going downward, and the

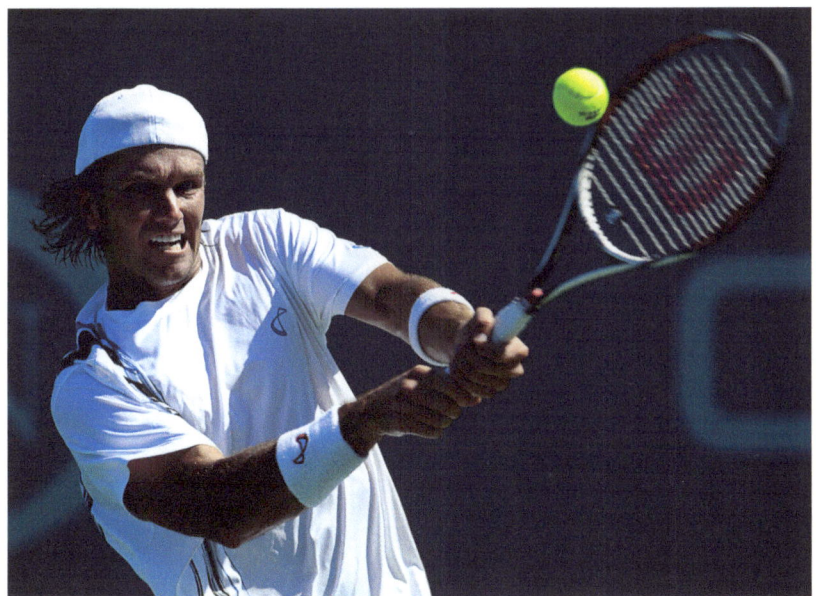

arms stick straight out in a rather odd-looking way. You can save yourself by quickly adjusting your composition to accommodate what could be a nice back-swing, especially if the player loops the racquet back up over his or her swing-shoulder. A forehand slice presents much the same problem, except the back-swing is hardly ever pretty.

The two-handed backhand can be one of the most dynamic-looking strokes to photograph.

FOLLOW-THROUGH

Follow-through photos can make nice profile shots — they contain just a little action, a little facial expression and a lot of concentration, while usually displaying the athlete's more usual-looking, non-contorted face. You may even capture wisps of hair or beads of perspiration flying through the air.

My favorite follow-through photo is of a two-handed backhand. The player will almost always hit this with top-spin, which means that the racquet will end up nicely tucked behind the head or over the shoulder. Both results can be used to frame the player's face while showing a bit of action, and he or she will usually have a focused expression.

A topspin forehand can also result in a nice follow-through, especially if the player is fundamentally sound. The racquet will again end up over the shoulder, or perhaps

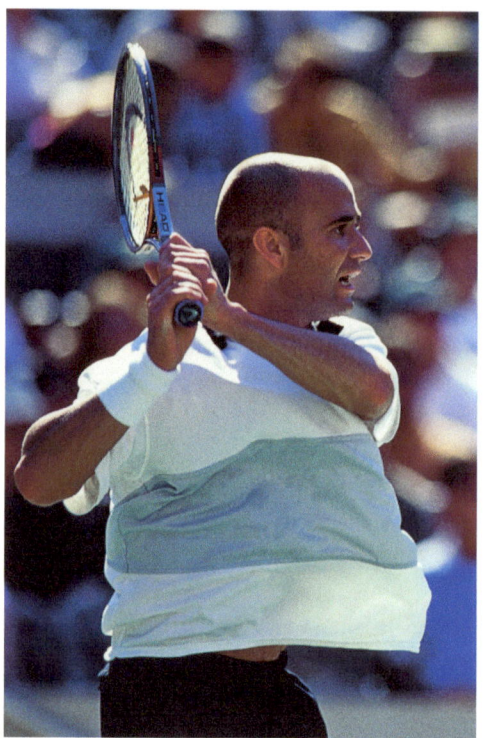

behind the head. Again, both options are relatively easy to compose nicely.

The follow-through of a one-handed topspin backhand can look very dynamic, but can also extend the player up so vertically that composing the frame becomes difficult. The trouble is that you end up with dead space at the sides of the image. If you try this shot, just be sure to leave room at the top for the racquet, or else it will fly out of your frame. Alternatively, follow-throughs of backspin strokes rarely photograph well, because the racquet usually ends up near the ground or protruding awkwardly from the player's form. Unless you need to docu-

The follow-through can yield a high-energy photograph, especially when clothing or hair is moving around.

ment swing mechanics (for instance, if you're shooting a sequence) or want an exercise in frustration, I wouldn't even bother photographing a backspin follow-through.

SERVE

Shooting serves can feel monotonous. There's little action and every player's mechanics are nearly identical to every other player's. But shoot them anyway—the opening shot of a point might be the only shot you get. Also, with different lenses you can be creative with different segments of the stroke.

Because the service motion has many different parts (from prep to toss to hit to follow-through) you have opportunities to make many types of images. No matter what you're trying for, though, keep in mind that a first serve will almost always be more aggressive than a second serve—the hit will be harder, the player will be moving faster. Therefore, know that a tightly composed subject will be harder to contain in the frame on the first serve than on the second.

Your first opportunity to shoot the serve is right before the toss, as the player bends down and stares intently toward the opponent. I like this moment, as it can show the intense focus that's unique to a professional athlete. However, it's also an easy image to make, so it takes only a frame or two to get the shot and move on. You'll also need to be creative to make it look original.

Next, consider shooting the toss. Remember that if the player can hear your camera, etiquette dictates waiting until after contact before shooting. But if the player can't hear you, or if you're in an environment where the player is accustomed to ignoring the noise of a shutter (such as at a big pro tournament), or if you're shooting someone who doesn't care (such as your friend or child), then capitalize on this moment. You can make very nice, even elegant, images during the service toss. Frame loose vertically, or tight horizontally, and try to time your shot to the ball just leaving the hand. Or frame vertically and shoot the player reaching and looking skyward, awaiting the tossed ball to fall. Either way, you'll probably want to pre-focus the image (i.e., lock in the focus before the action starts, then frame your composition) and wait for the perfect moment to shoot.

Capturing the serve at contact isn't any harder than shooting any other stroke at contact, but composing it can be more difficult because there's so much body motion. The most frequently successful strategy is framing the player's head and shoulders at the bottom of the composition and leaving room for the racquet and ball in the top half.

The tennis serve has a certain elegance that's unmatched in other parts of the game. Combined with great light and a solid composition, you can make some pretty images.

Shooting after contact can also make for an interesting photo. I love trying to capture the wrist pronating, freezing the tennis player's arm while it's contorting in a way that's not apparent to the naked eye, a body movement unique to the sport. Composing pronation can be challenging,

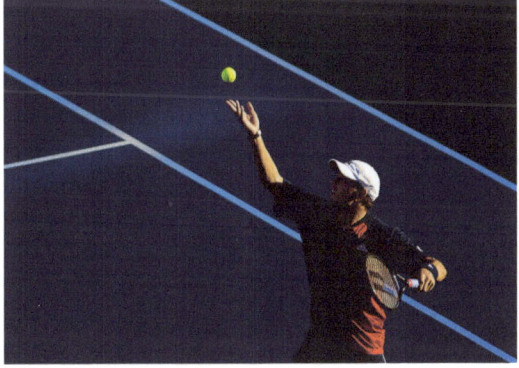

but also rewarding. There's a bit of a wow-factor to this photo for a viewer who appreciates athleticism.

One tip for shooting a serve after contact: The player will be falling from their highest reach. Don't try to follow with the lens, because you're almost certain to over- or under-adjust. Instead, anticipate the space he or she will fall into. Compensate drastically—crop the head off (as if you're shooting just the torso) and then let the player fall into your frame. (See the photo on page 101.)

Though the serve presents opportunities for so many different types of images at different moments, you can't do them all in one service motion. The setup for each shot is completely different, requiring different orientation, framing and even lenses. But don't worry—you'll have plenty of opportunities for all these options throughout the match.

SERVICE RETURN

Because returns are often just a player "blocking" the ball back to the server, you often don't see much of a back-stroke, much of a follow-through, or much dynamic action in between. Your best bet for a great photograph is if the server fools the receiver, causing him or her to have to lunge for the ball. Thus, your best shot will frequently be a tightly-framed photo, whether vertical or horizontal.

Service returns, particularly on the first serve, can draw the returning player into a quick burst of action.

You'll have more opportunities during a second serve. Because of the shot's less aggressive nature, the returner will usually be in a better position to make a more fundamentally sound shot back. However, for the same reason,

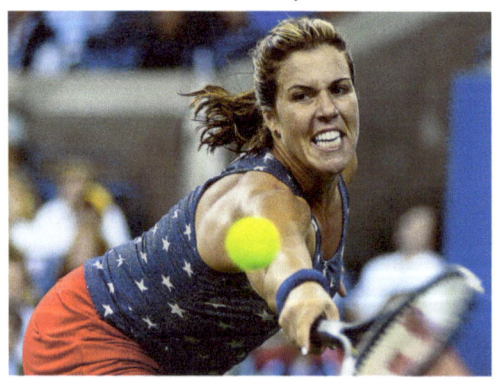

you'll hardly ever get a chance to make a *dynamic* photo during the second serve. The exception is if the server is a heavy hitter—Andy Roddick, for instance, is plenty capable of whacking a "safe" second serve at 130 miles per hour. That's plenty fast enough to elicit a photographically exciting return.

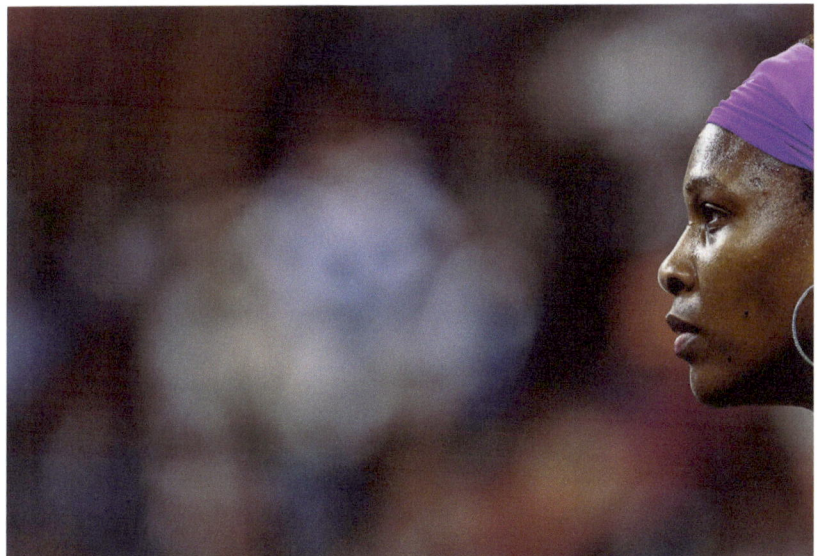

The return will also give you a chance to shoot some between-point moments. The returner will usually play with the racquet, align strings, adjust clothing and so on, all while looking very focused.

VOLLEY

I found getting photos at net to be easier in the 1990s than I did in the 2000s. And I imagine photographers in the 1970s and 1980s found it easier still. Why? Because as the decades pass, fewer players hit volleys. They just don't come to net much anymore.

The volley is also one of the more difficult strokes to photograph. The problem is that you need to be *ready* to shoot it. You usually can't have your camera trained at the baseline and then just switch to the net when the player runs in. You would probably need to change lenses mid-point, which just isn't practical in tennis. Even if you were working with two camera bodies with different lenses mounted, you still wouldn't have time to switch. The only instance in which I bother trying to move my focus from baseline to net is if I'm shooting from behind the court, across the net. Even then, it's really only possible with a telephoto zoom lens — in fact, this strategy is perhaps the best use in tennis

Pay attention to the player awaiting serve, who is often uniquely focused and intense. You might feel as if it's too easy a photo to make, but finding ways to be creative can be rewarding.

for the 200-400mm f/4 (on a camera with a magnification factor of 1.5x or greater).

If you want to shoot volleys, you generally have to be *trying* to. You need to choose your lens and your angle with this purpose in mind, and then abandon much thought of getting good photos of other strokes.

The easiest spot to shoot volleys from is perpendicular to the net, which you can do only if positioned at the end of the court. From there you can shoot volleys no matter which side the player moves toward, all while probably being able to keep the background clean. Again, this position requires a good telephoto lens, i.e. a 300mm or 400mm.

A more interesting angle is from the side, about even with the net (if you have a large enough aperture to blur the background distractions — and from that angle there will be many). You can also situate yourself about even with the service line and shoot toward the opposite side of the net. From both those spots, a 70-200mm lens (or something thereabouts) will grant the visual latitude you'll need for the myriad possibilities of what could happen once a player approaches for a volley. Also, if you want to shoot the player

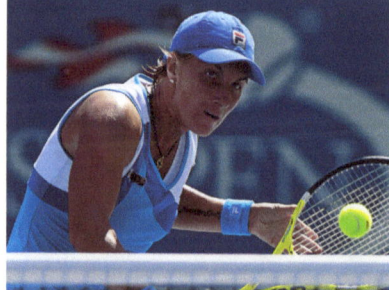

actually hitting the ball, he or she will need to be moving toward your side of the court. Otherwise the action will be going away from the camera and you'd just be shooting their backside. In that case, wait until after the volley is hit, and then the player will probably look back toward you; if the ball is coming directly at you, you may even be able to

The easiest way to shoot a volley is from the backcourt, shooting across the net, straight at the player.

photograph the player looking across the net toward you and the ball.

A few other things to know about shooting volleys:

1. If you're shooting from courtside with your lens aimed at the baseline, and you want to *try* to adjust to shoot a volley, then know that your light level will likely change by as much as a full stop. Therefore, you need to be ready to re-aim the camera, adjust your framing and change exposure

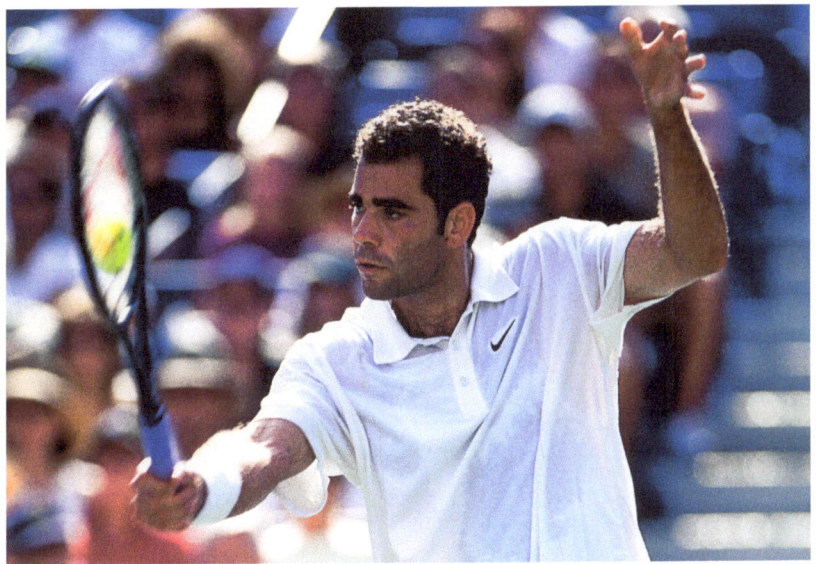

all in the same half second. To make this easier, predetermine your net exposure so you can dial it in quickly (similar to the technique described in "Shooting in Mixed Light" on page 84).

2. Net play happens very fast, so you need equally fast reactions to photograph it. A camera with no discernible shutter lag is almost a necessity.

3. A volley photo almost always works better as a horizontal, because the action is happening horizontally. Trying to frame a volley vertically usually results in dead space at one side and in two or three of the corners of the frame.

It's not easy, and you have to be patient and knowledgeable about the player's tendencies, but you can photograph a volley with a short-telephoto zoom lens from courtside near the net. Use a small aperture to keep the background out of focus.

As mentioned before, modern tennis players don't come to net often, so trying to shoot volleys results in a very low yield of good photos. You could dedicate an entire match to trying to shoot volleys and not get one successful image. To increase your odds of success, know which players employ a serve-and-volley game, and learn when they come to net. This might be the area of tennis photography where it's most useful to understand how the game is played, so that you can predict when net play will happen.

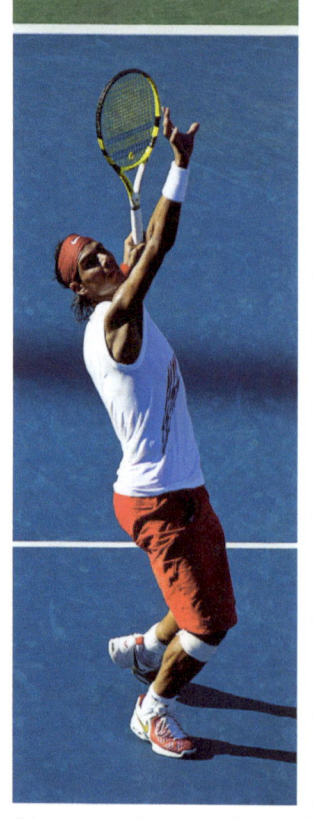

If you want to practice shooting volleys in a live game, try to find a doubles match, where more than half the action takes place at the net.

OVERHEAD

Overheads are even harder to photograph than volleys, due again to a lack of frequency. Unless you're in position to shoot a volley, then you're probably not in position to shoot an overhead. You're really never *waiting* to shoot one, unless for some reason it's the only shot you're trying for. The one advantage you have is because the ball is high, you usually have time to adjust.

Another problem with shooting overheads is that they generally look exactly like a serve, but with less energy. The only really good overhead images are when the player leaps for the shot, which is rare. You can also get a decent photo of a backhand overhead, but that's even more rare. If you get a good photo of a leaping backhand overhead, call the Pulitzer board and claim your prize.

Trying to capture an overhead at contact presents a compositional problem as well, because the

About the only place I like shooting overheads is from over-head. The mechanics usually look just like a serve, but from up top you can see the player is not at the service line.

player will be stretched out very vertically, meaning you'll have a lot of empty background in the frame. In fact, the only player I can remember looking really good during the overhead is Pete Sampras. The leaping overhead was one of his signature shots, and his form was very dynamic. Of course, Sampras is now retired.

If none of this has scared you away, then go ahead and attack the overhead with a short telephoto lens (from the side) or a 300mm (from straight-on). And try to find Sampras at a senior match.

LOB & DROP SHOT

Both are generally terrible to shoot. The mechanics required to hit either shot just don't look good in a photograph. My advice is that if you're tracking a player who's about to hit either a lob or drop shot, quickly swing your focus toward the other side of the court. If either shot is hit well, then the opponent will have to scramble, which can often look dynamic. Also, a well-placed drop shot will draw the opponent toward the net. You could find ample opportunity to shoot him or her in a furious run directly at your position, and lunging for the ball. A well-placed lob could fare the photographer even better—it's sometimes the precursor to a between-the-legs shot (see page 138).

If a player starts hitting moon balls (high defensive lobs that some fans and players deem unsportsmanlike), then don't even bother shooting. The back-swing will look terrible, as will the follow-through, and then the player will just look up out of the frame. Shoot the opponent instead. You might get a photo of him or her looking annoyed. Turn toward the other photographers, or the crowd, for the same reaction.

APPROACH SHOT

Approach shots don't always look the same—they're just a general term for a stroke that you might have to hit when moving from the baseline to the net. I group them into their own category because they have something in common: They're difficult to photograph well.

Approach shots usually bring a player low to the ground so he or she can hit right after the ball bounces. But sometimes the player will stay high enough to make a good photo.

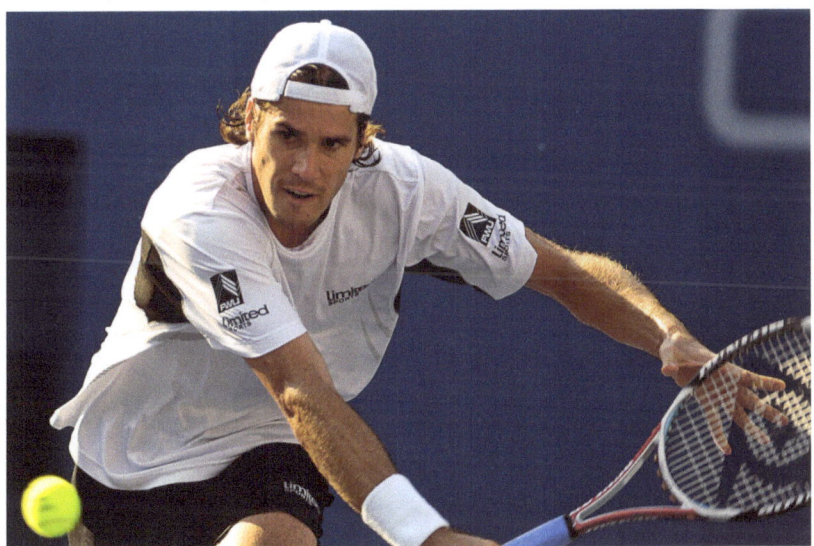

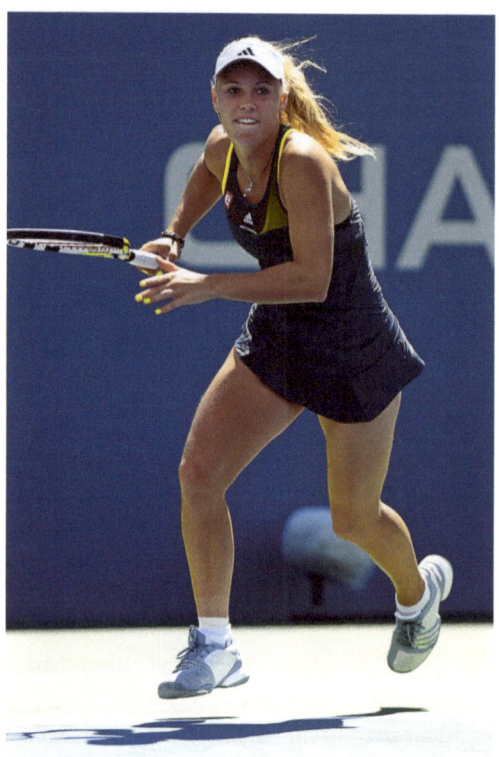

Most often, a player has to move low to the ground to hit an approach shot, which means he or she will be crouching. This usually means you have to adjust your framing quickly. It also usually involves a transition between focal lengths; that's easy enough if you have a normal-to-short-telephoto zoom lens on the camera, but not otherwise.

Also, you can usually photograph an approach shot only from the end of the court or from the sidelines near center court, on the same side as the player you're targeting. If you're sitting elsewhere, either the player's back will be to your camera, or the net or net post will obstruct your view. If you do find yourself in the right position with the right lens, just be patient. Because the action is speeding up on court, your adrenaline-induced instinct may be to fire the shutter prematurely. But wait until you know the ball is coming. It's tricky timing, and it's a low-yield opportunity. But it can also be a chance for some unique and rewarding images.

Any time a player is pulled out of position, he or she may have to run for the next shot.

RUNNING

One of my favorite non-ball action photos is of players running.

Tennis is a game of footwork, wherein speed isn't quite as important as moving the feet in a way that keeps your momentum flexible. Therefore, you won't usually see players break into a full run. Even when they do, it will be a quick sprint, which will leave you little time to react. Therefore, as with so many other aspects of tennis photography, if you want to photograph a player running then you need to be able to predict when he or she will run. Even better is if you can predict when the player will run right toward you. That's usually the most dynamic angle.

If you want to shoot a player on the run, look for these signs that it's about to happen:

- If you are positioned near the baseline and the player has to chase a wide shot on the other side of the court from you, then, to get back in position, he or she will probably stop, pivot and run back toward you. This is a great opportunity to photograph the run because the player will be coming right at the camera. Just beware that you may need to control a messy background.

- If you're shooting from the end of the court, watch for your subject's opponent (who will be on your side of the net) to hit a short reply, such as a drop shot. The player you're focused on will have to run toward the net, which is toward you.

When shooting from behind the court, watch for your subject's opponent to hit a drop shot. This creates a nice opportunity to photograph the player running directly toward you.

- If a player has to chase a deep shot, you probably won't be able to shoot the run, because he or she will likely be heading away from you. The only time this won't be true is if you're shooting from the end of the court on the same side as the player who's chasing the ball—then the player is running right at you. But in that case, you probably would have been aiming at the far court with a long telephoto lens that can't focus on the closer player. You would be able

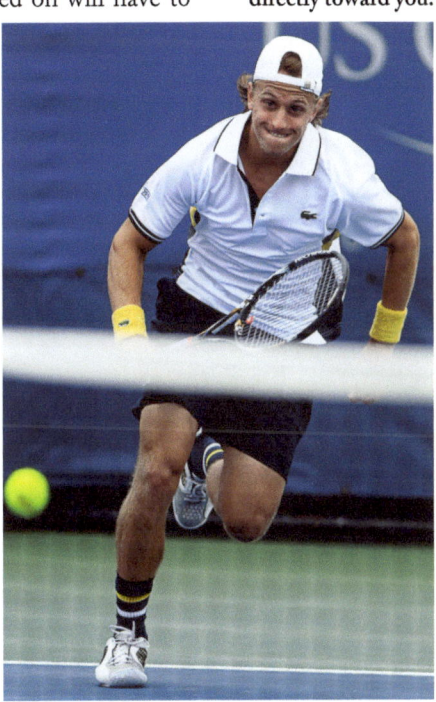

take advantage of this position only if you have a normal or wide-angle lens mounted, in which case you can make a *great* photo while the player runs toward you with the court and the rest of the tennis environment in the background.

BETWEEN-THE-LEGS

The between-the-legs shot is arguably the most dynamic in tennis. You hardly ever see good images of one, because it's so rare that many photographers either don't know how to watch for it or just forget to.

Here's the trick: The player has to be at net, and the opponent has to hit a lob very far back in the court. Put that scenario in your head—file it under "wake up if I see it happen"—because this is when to watch for the possibility of a between-the-legs shot.

The more the player has to run back to chase down the lob, the more likely he or she will try to hit between the legs. (Assuming that the player is prone to try this shot anyway. Most aren't.) If you can see that the player is running

The only way to predict a between-the-legs shot is to know in what situation it might happen and whether the player is nervy enough to try it.

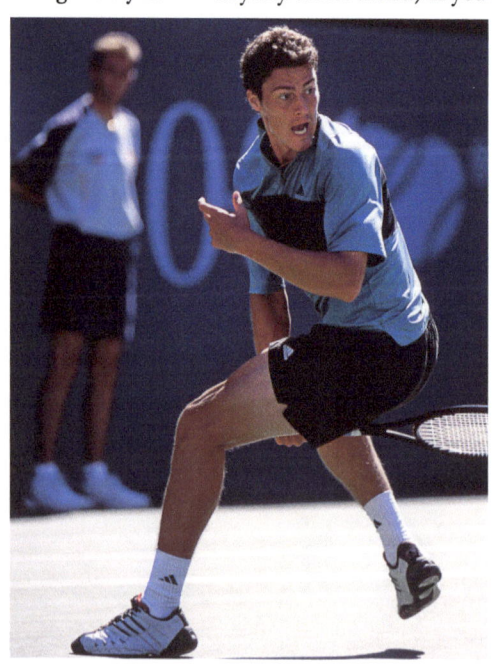

directly toward the ball rather than to a spot next to the ball, then you can be almost certain he or she will hit between the legs. Once you see the possibility arise, don't panic. The tendency here is to just trip the shutter as soon as you see the shot developing. But wait. Be patient.

If you're shooting perpendicular to the action, your best opportunity may be at impact or immediately after. However, you'll rarely be in that spot. More likely, you'll be at an angle to the player's back, in which case his or her head will be facing away from you. If you

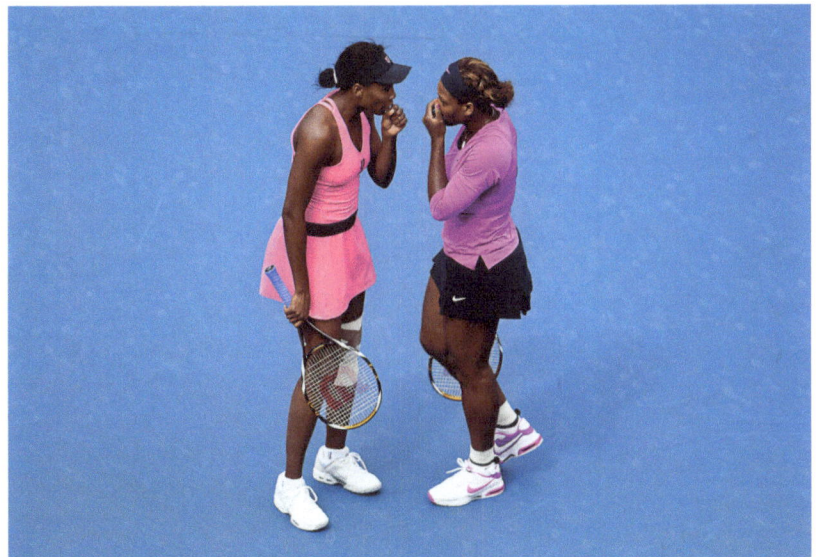

don't have the player's face, then you *need* to get the ball in the frame, otherwise it's just a photo of a back. Therefore, shoot either at impact or immediately after.

Once the ball has been hit, the player will look over the shoulder to see where it went. That instant can also make for a good photo, as the racquet will still be between the legs. Therefore, pick your moment to shoot the action, then fire twice—once for the ball, once for the look. Then stay locked on the player. If the shot is a winner, you'll get a great reaction; if not, you should still get a smile.

DOUBLES

So far this book has discussed tennis photos in terms of shooting singles play. However, tennis supplies a whole other world of opportunities in doubles.

You can use a doubles match as an opportunity to shoot four players doing their own thing. In other words, doubles provides twice as many people to make solo photos of in one match. If you're trying to build a catalog of player photos, doubles can double your pace. However, this advantage is offset by the fact that each player will hit only half the balls struck to his or her side of the court, so the player you track will not always be participating in the action. How do

Between-point conferences can relay the sense of teamwork unique to doubles play.

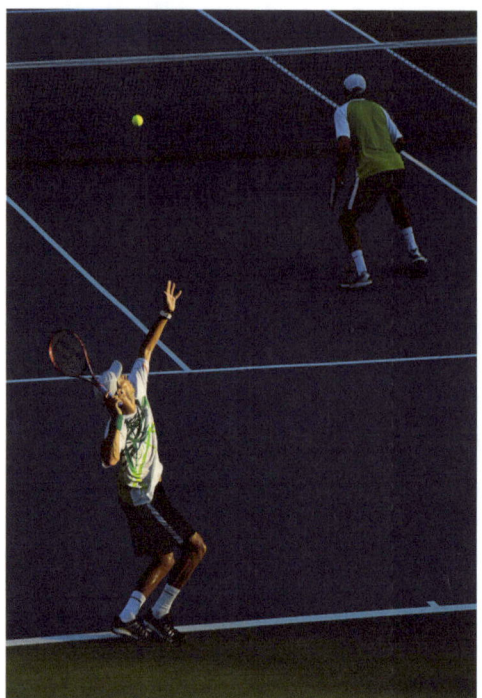

you know whom to focus on? Knowledge of the game will help, but even then it's a guess. You just have to pick a player and stick to your decision until there's a chance or a reason to change your mind.

Alternatively, doubles can also provide a unique aesthetic to tennis photos. Four people are on court at once. If you can get them all in the same composition, you can make some interesting images. To do this effectively is hard; I rarely see a good doubles photo that includes all four players. When successful, photos like this are usually made from behind the ends of the court.

Shooting doubles allows for compositions that are not possible in the singles game.

What's more common, and just as unique to doubles, is to shoot action of both members of a team playing together during a point. This is easier than composing a photo of four players, but still more difficult than shooting just one. Another difficulty is getting both players in focus. Because you're usually photographing tennis with large apertures (to facilitate high shutter speeds), you're working with very shallow depth of field. Therefore, try to use selective-focus techniques for artistic effect, or find moments when you don't need such a quick shutter.

Another dynamic unique to doubles is teamwork. You can illustrate this nicely in photographs by shooting the players celebrating together or conferring between points.

REACTIONS & MOMENTS

This is Sports Photography 101, but I often see photographers of all levels persistently ignoring this dictum: Don't stop shooting just because the point is over.

When the action stops, that's when you can make some

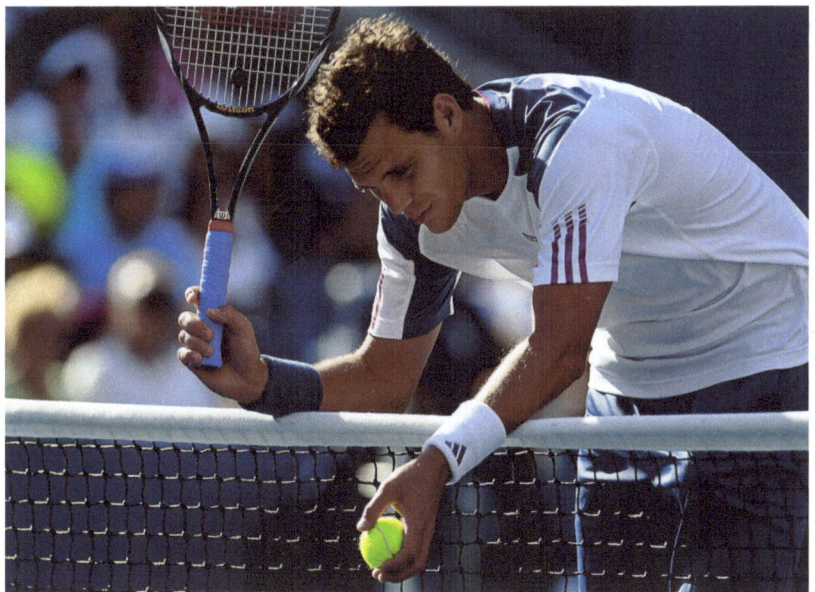

of your best tennis photos. That's when you can shoot players reacting to winners and errors, responding to great moments. They yell. They smile. They smash racquets. They contemplate. They look to the sky, to the coach, to the parent, to the girlfriend sitting courtside. They call the trainer, they change racquets, they towel off their perspiration. All of this is great fodder for great photographs.

So when the point ends, stay focused on the player. Most of the time—probably 98 percent—you'll get nothing. Yes, that's a low-yield strategy. But that two percent can net you some of your best images.

You can improve your percentages by paying close attention to the match. When peering through the peephole of a telephoto lens, following forehand after forehand and backhand after backhand and return after serve, you can lull yourself into forgetting the score. Don't let that happen. Know what's at stake for the players from point to point and game to game, because that will tell you when they may laugh, cheer, or break a racquet on the court. The end of a set, the end of a tie-break, the end of a long deuce game, the end of a particularly long and difficult rally—all of these are moments that you can expect to be followed by some out-of-the-ordinary expression from a player.

Life doesn't stop just because a point is over. Never take your camera off the player until you're positive there's nothing left to photograph. Otherwise you'll miss moments like this.

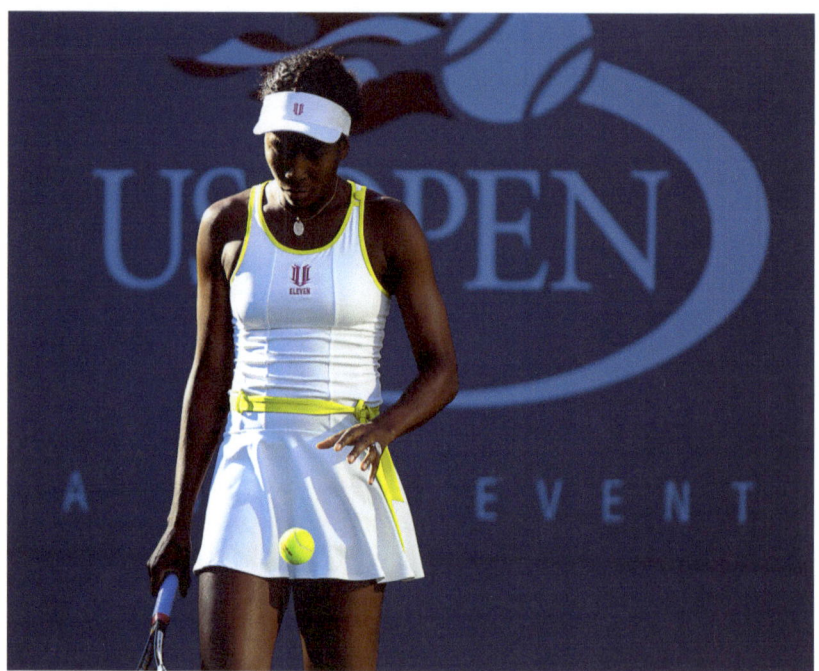

Look for quiet moments in a match, when players may appear pensive, or tired, or determined.

The end of a match is the most obvious time to shoot for emotional reactions. But match-winning points can actually be anticlimactic if they were preceded by emotionally draining games or points. If a player celebrates winning a long, grueling return game to take a 6-5 lead in the final set, you may see a bigger reaction at that moment than when he or she easily serves out for a 7-5 victory.

If you're at a big tournament and want to maximize your chances to shoot these moments, watch the scoreboards. Look for matches that are close to ending. Look for possible upsets. Go to those courts and await the result. You might get better photos by hunting down these opportunities than by camping at one court and shooting a hundred more ground strokes.

Of course, other between-point moments happen, too. Some players show great personalities on court. They may goof around with the ballkids, make funny faces, interact with a fan, argue with an umpire. These moments are hard to predict and can be difficult to react to quickly. (Again, tennis can lull a photographer into tunnel vision.) My advice for these situations is that if you think something quirky might

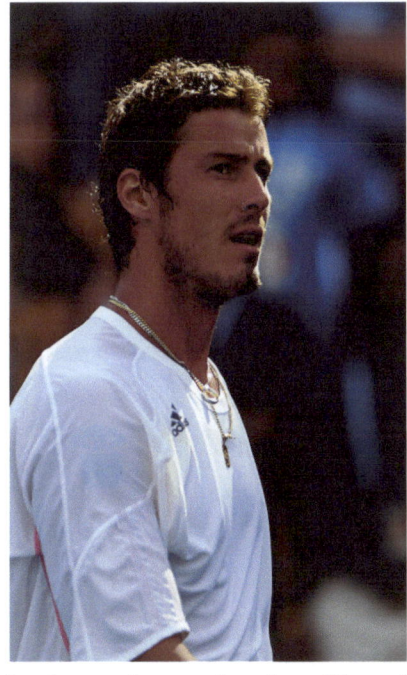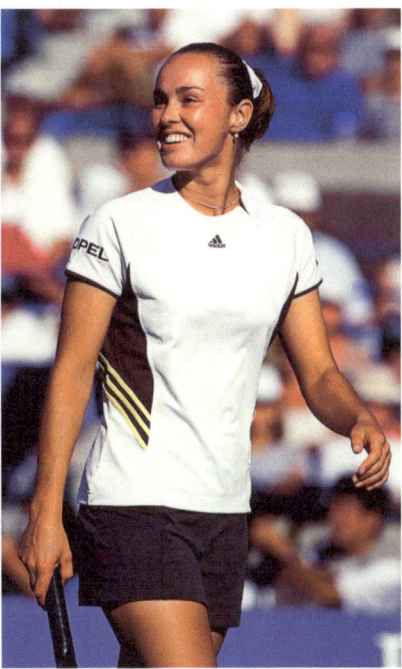

be about to happen, just shoot. If your hunch is wrong, you can delete the file; if right, you pad your portfolio. You'll get a lot of junk, but at least you won't miss the fun stuff.

AMBIANCE

Tennis, especially at a tournament, is not about just the play. There's an atmosphere and a lifestyle on display, much of which can make for fascinating photography.

If you find yourself shooting professionals or aspiring pros, then you're photographing some of the world's elite athletes. Hone in on their body parts—show the muscles, the tone, the strength, the conditioning. Or focus on the gear—close-ups of bags, racquet strings, vibration dampers, or balls, or shoes, or shoelaces. Photographically, you can almost always break down a scene into its parts, each of which can be its own subject.

Look for other things going on, too. The environment of a tennis match is comprised of more than just players. What are the ballkids doing? How about the line and chair umpires, the security guards, the ushers, the fans? Is rain is

Watch for players exhibiting any kind of emotion. Usually they appear blank, so catching them in a moment of intensity, frustration or joy can make for good photography.

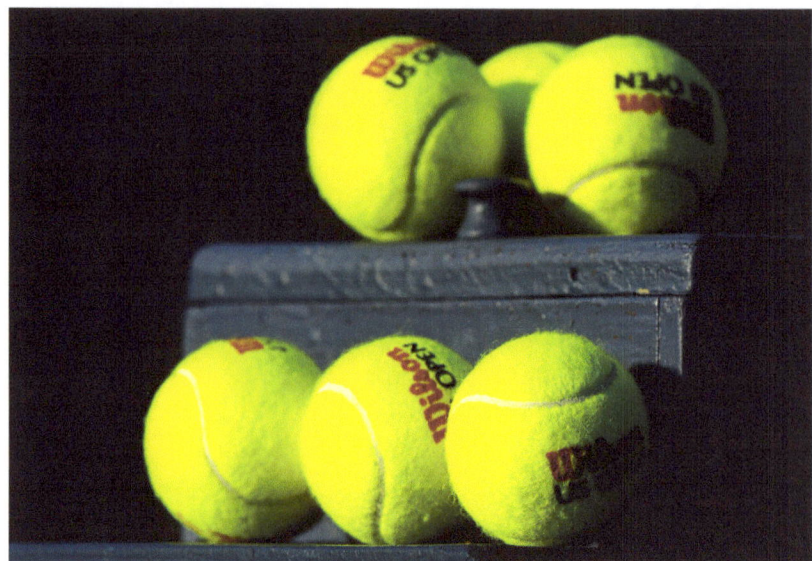

Keep your eyes trained off the court, too. You'll likely see possibilities for images that tell a tennis story just as well as a great action shot does.

delaying play? Shoot the reflections in the court puddles, the umbrellas in the stands, the grounds crew sluicing the water from the courts with squeegees.

Look away from the courts, too. Tournaments are often a flurry of activity. Look for interesting scenes of people at the food court, or warm light playing across the tournament signage, of kids enjoying a day out with Mom or Dad.

Yes, shooting tennis can be hard. But the good news is that great photo opportunities constantly surround you. You can't spend one minute at a tennis event without seeing something worthy of a photograph.

APPENDIX

ONLINE RESOURCES

WWW.PHOTOGRAPHINGTENNIS.COM
The website for this book. Read additional tips and view a list of professional tournaments where you can photograph the action.

ITPA CODE OF CONDUCT
Whether or not they're making money with photography, all tennis photographers should conduct themselves according to these guidelines issued by the International Tennis Photographers Association. Visit www.tennisphotographers.com/Conduct.htm.

BEST PRACTICES FOR BUSINESS
If you have any interest in making money off even one of your photos, protect yourself and the industry by ensuring you do it the right way. The American Society of Media Photographers (www.asmp.org) and Editorial Photographers (www.editorialphoto.com) are excellent resources.

WWW.ROBGALBRAITH.COM
An invaluable resource for researching the best memory cards to use with your camera. A vast database reports the write speed of just about every card on the market when used with just about every camera.

WWW.LUMINOUS-LANDSCAPE.COM
Loads of accessible information about the trends and developments in digital imaging technology and the new issues it brings to photography. Especially note the articles about how lens diffraction can reduce your camera's resolution, and how to "expose to the right" (ETTR) for better image quality.

WWW.KENROCKWELL.COM

A valuable, unbiased resource for information on camera models and their technical specifications.

WWW.SPORTSSHOOTER.COM

An online community of professional, student and serious-amateur sports photographers. A good resource for equipment reviews (as the gear relates to action photography), advice on working in various venues, info on workshops and more.

RULE OF THIRDS

For a tutorial on the compositional "Rule of Thirds," visit www.cambridgeincolour.com/tutorials/rule-of-thirds.htm.

INDEX

P

peripheral vision 120
photo pit 4, 5
photo vest 43
point of highest contrast 63, 102, 110
point & shoot camera 21
polarizing filter 39, 40, 41, 55
positioning 46, 47, 52, 63
professionalism 2, 65
public courts 57, 84

Q

quick-release plates 34

R

reactions 140, 141
resolution 11, 12, 145
Roddick, Andy 130
rule of thirds 16, 17, 18, 104, 108, 146
rules (tennis) 117
running 99, 135, 136

S

Sampras, Pete 2, 21, 89, 134
second serve 130
selective focus 113, 140
Seles, Monica xii, 106
sensor 11, 12, 13, 23, 24, 75
sequences 19, 38
serve 3, 101, 128, 129, 130
service return 130
service toss 129
shadows 55, 68, 69, 70, 72, 74, 75, 77, 99
short-telephoto zoom lens 23, 136
shutter lag 13, 14, 16, 119
shutter release 14, 15, 18, 88, 96, 116
shutter speed 26, 28, 29, 32, 68, 72, 79, 80, 82, 83, 85, 86
side courts 52, 53
side light 55, 70
Sigma 23
sound blimp 20, 43
sound (timing) 117, 119
strobe 7, 21
sunlight 84, 85, 86

T

Tamrac 43
target resolution 12
teleconverter 26, 27, 28
telephoto lens 22, 31, 32, 51, 60, 64, 96, 114, 132, 137, 141
telephoto zoom lens 23, 133, 136
television cameras 47, 59, 62, 63
tendonitis 88
third-stops 82
timing 15, 16, 96, 97, 102, 116, 117, 119, 123, 126, 136
top light 55, 68
tournament logos 59, 62
tripod 34
Twizzlers 42
two-handed backhand 126, 127

U

umpire chair 63
US Open xii, 3, 5, 118
UV filter 41

V

value (of photos) 8
variable-aperture lens 27, 29
vertical grip 88
video camera 43
viewfinder 38, 116, 120, 122
volleys 131, 133

W

warming filter 41
white balance 73
wide-angle lens 25, 52, 99
wide-angle zoom lens 43
Williams, Venus 69
windscreen 53, 74
write speed 36, 145

X

Xrite ColorChecker 73

Z

zoom lens 23, 25, 27, 29, 131, 133, 136

www.ingramcontent.com/pod-product-compliance
Lightning Source LLC
Chambersburg PA
CBHW040820180526
45159CB00001B/12